More Praise for *Twelve Months of Monastery Soups*

"My vocation may be talking about money, but my avocation is cooking, and soups are my passion. Brother Victor-Antoine's recipes are a joy to make and healthy for both your body and your wallet."

—Doria Dolan, Financial Contributor,
"CBS This Morning"

"Modern science has begun to appreciate the age-old wisdom of a diet focused more on vegetables and less on meat. Yet how do we find the time to cook these dishes? Surely a hot soup ranks as the easiest and tastiest way to do so. Brother Victor-Antoine offers us nearly 200 variations on this theme. They all provide abundant servings of the vegetables we so greatly need. This work will help lead many back to a simpler, healthier cuisine!"

—Jon J. Michnovicz, M.D., Ph.D., President and Medical
Director of the Foundation for Preventive Oncology;
author of *How to Reduce Your Risk of Breast Cancer*

"Brother Victor-Antoine is a plain cook only in the sense that he uses ordinary ingredients in season, grown in the garden of the monastery in New York State. He combines vegetables with little fuss or fanfare, counting on the flavors themselves rather than an extremely complicated process to work the magic. . . . This book has been an education for me."

—*Greenville Herald Banner*

"A history of monastery soups blends with exciting seasonal recipes in a blend of culinary history and cookbook. . . . Most recipes are quick and easy to reproduce and will appeal to many readers in their simplicity."

—*Midwest Book Review*

Twelve Months of Monastery Soups

Brother Victor-Antoine d'Avila-Latourrette

BROADWAY BOOKS

New York

BROADWAY

A hardcover edition of this book was originally published in 1996 by Triumph™ Books, An Imprint of Liguori Publications. It is here reprinted by arrangement with Triumph™ Books.

Broadway Books titles may be purchased for business or promotional use or for special sales. For information, please write to: Special Markets Department, Bantam Doubleday Dell Publishing Group, Inc., 1540 Broadway, New York, NY 10036.

BROADWAY BOOKS and its logo, a letter B bisected on the diagonal, are trademarks of Broadway Books, a division of Bantam Doubleday Dell Publishing Group, Inc.

First Broadway Books trade paperback edition published 1998.

Library of Congress Cataloging-in-Publication Data
D'Avila-Latourrette, Victor-Antoine.
    Twelve months of monastery soups : international favorites /
  Brother Victor-Antoine d'Avila-Latourrette.
        p.   cm.
    Reprint. Originally published: Liguori, MO : Triumph Books, 1996.
    Includes index.
    ISBN 0-7679-0180-0 (pbk.)
    1. Soups.   2. Vegetarian cookery.   3. Cookery, International.
  I. Title.
TX757.D36   1998
641.8'13—dc21   97-42099
                                                              CIP

03 04 05   10

To my dear friends and neighbors
Lucy and Wigbold Van Limburg Stirum
and Silvia Koner,
who with their loyal friendship encouraged me
to bring this work to a successful completion

Contents

Preface 1

Ingredients and Substitutions 3

January

Saint Basil Soup 6

Chickpea Soup à la Provençale 7

Mushroom Soup à la Marie-Louise 8

Caldo Verde (Portuguese Cabbage Soup) 9

Artichoke and Potato Soup 10

Cream of Pea Soup 11

Brussels Sprout Soup 12

Orzo Soup 13

Saint Antony Soup 14

Velouté à la Dubarry (Cauliflower Velouté) 15

Cotriade Bretonne (Fish Soup from Brittany) 16

Cherbah (Arabic Soup) 17

Black-Eyed Pea Soup 18

Spicy English Parsnip Soup 19

Spinach Cream Soup 20

February

Potage de Navets (Turnip Soup) 22

Saint Scholastica Soup 23

French Lentil Soup 24

Garlic Royale 25

Polish Pearl Barley Soup 26

Quick Black Bean Mexican Soup 27

Escarole and Bean Minestra 28

Old-fashioned Cream of Leek Provençal Soup 29

Bouillabaisse à la Marseillaise 30

Country Mushroom and Sour Cream Soup 32

Soupe du Berry (Red Bean Soup from Berry) 33

Ravioli Potage 34

Cheese Velouté 35

Bulgarian Soup 36

March

Saint Lioba Beer and Mushroom Soup 38

Spicy Indian Soup 39

Basic Onion Soup 40

Minestrone di Verdura (Tuscan Green Vegetable Minestrone) 41

Everyday Potato Soup 42

Garlic Soup 43

Lima Bean Soup 44

Béguine Cream Soup 45

Bread and Milk Soup 46

Fava Bean Soup 47

Watercress Soup 48

Saint Patrick Irish Cheddar Soup 49

Harrira (Moroccan Bean Soup) 50

Butternut Squash Soup Portuguese Style 51

Soup Julienne 52

April

Cream of Mushroom Soup à la Romaine 54

Sweet Milk Soup for Children 55

Potage Villageois (Village Vegetable-
  Macaroni Soup) 56

Borscht 57

Sour Cream Soup 58

Potage Germiny (Sorrel Soup) 59

Cream of Curry Potage 60

Shrimp Soup de Luxe 61

Three Peppers Soup 62

Cream of Asparagus Soup 63

Saint Joseph Chickpea Soup 64

Cuban Black Bean Soup 65

Vermicelli Soup 66

Brussels Sprout Cream Potage 67

May

Russian *Chtchavel* 70

Potage Clamart (Turnip-Leek Potage) 71

Shaker-Style Soup 72

Asparagus-Orange Velouté 73

Cabbage Soup 74

Potage Céline (Carrot-Celeriac Soup) 75

Cream of Broccoli Soup 76

Irish Brotchan Soup 77

Minestrone Monastico 78

Potage Printanier à la Française
  (French Spring Vegetable Soup) 79

Saint Germain Pea Soup 80

Avocado Velouté 81

Saint Christopher Soup 82

June

Soup from the Ardennes 84

Cream of Fresh Greens Soup 85

Oyster and Mushroom Soup 86

Danish Onion–Champagne Soup 87

Potato Dumpling Soup 88

Greek Spartan Soup 89

Chervil Soup 90

Solyanka (Cucumber-Fish Soup) 91

Cream of Cauliflower Soup 92

Zuppa di Pasta e Fagioli (Pasta and
  Bean Soup) 93

Carrot Soup à la Normande 94

Exotic Chinese Cucumber Soup 95

Spanish Cilantro Soup 96

Celery-Orange Velouté 97

Chilled Carrot Soup 98

July

Saint Bertille Herb Soup 100

Cream of Vegetable Soup à la Mode
  de Tours 101

Consommé of Celeriac 102

Jerusalem Artichoke Soup	103
Colbert Clear Soup	104
Cold Tomato Soup	105
Shrimp and Corn Chowder	106
Consommé Madrilène	107
Avocado Soup	108
Cold Salmon Chowder	109
Pea and Carrot Minted Soup	110
Neapolitan Zucchini Soup	111
Cold Basil Soup	112

August

Cream of Fennel Soup	114
Garlic Consommé	115
Broccoli Soup	116
Soupe Pelou (Radish Greens Soup)	117
Parsley Soup	118
Gazpacho	119
Garden Borscht	120
Consommé Belle Fermière (Farmer Vegetable Soup)	121
Potage Crécy (Carrot Potage)	122
Cold Zucchini Soup	123
Spicy Carrot and Orange Soup	124
Wild Rice Soup	125

September

Cream of Celery Soup	128
Monastery Quick Vichyssoise	129

Potage du Jardin (Garden Vegetable Soup)	130
Russian Cream of String Bean Soup	131
Tomato Bouillon	132
Cream of Corn Soup	133
Tomato Soup Florentine Style	134
Fennel, Zucchini, and Tomato Soup	135
Provençal Rainbow Soup	136
Gumbo Potage à la Creole	137
Curried Soybean Soup	138
Minestra Toscana (Tuscan-Style Minestrone)	139
Escarole Soup	140
Red Bean and Rice Soup	141

October

Brodo alla Romana (Broth Roman Style)	144
Spinach Soup	145
Pasta and Lentil Soup	146
Traditional Austrian Cheese Soup	147
Saint Seraphim Soup	148
Soupe Savoyarde (Savoyard Cream of Potato Soup)	149
Ossobuco Soup	150
Southern-Style Vegetable Soup	151
Beet Soup	152
Soupe au Pistou (Provençal Vegetable Soup with Pesto Sauce)	153
Leek and Potato Soup	154
French Cream of Lentil Soup	155
Corn Soup	156

November

Okra Soup	158
Potage au Potiron (Pumpkin Soup)	159
Portuguese Kale Soup	160
Black Bean Soup	161
Potato and Cheese Soup	162
White Bean Soup	163
Broccoli Rabe and Bean Soup	164
Zuppa alla Pavese (Bread Soup from Pavia)	165
Rice and Ham Soup	166
Garbure Béarnaise (Béarn Country Soup)	167
Swiss Chard and Lentil Soup	168
Basic Monastic Garlic Soup	169
Potage à l'Oseille (Cream of Sorrel Soup)	170

December

Aigo-Boulido (Herb Bouillon)	172
Saint Nicholas Soup	173
Zuppa Toscana (Tuscan Bread and Tomato Soup)	174
Saint Lucy Soup Sicilian Style	175
Yellow Pea Soup	176
Caldo Gallego (Galician Chickpea and Sausage Soup)	177
A Hermit's Soup	178

Simple Onion Soup	179
Zuppa Vesubio (Vesuvio Vegetable-Cheese Soup)	180
Soybean Minestra	181
Gloucester English Cheese Soup	182
Beer Soup	183
Acorn Squash Soup	184
Egg Soup	185
Mushroom Soup	186
Potage aux Deux Légumes (Celery-Carrot Soup)	187

Appendix
Basic Recipes for Stocks, Sauces, and Croutons

Meat Broth	190
Consommé	191
Vegetable Broth	192
Chicken Broth	193
Fish Broth	193
White Sauce	194
Béchamel Sauce	194
Croutons	195
Index	197

Preface

Eat soup first and eat it last,
and live till a hundred years be past.
— French Proverb

From antiquity on, soups have always held a very prominent place in the daily fare of monasteries. This is still true today, particularly in French monasteries, where soup is often served twice a day, for the *déjeuner* (lunch) and, even more appropriately, for the *souper,* as the evening meal is called in France. The appeal of soup is universal; it seems to be almost of a basic instinctual nature. Soups are always welcome at any time of the year: hot during the cold weather months and cold during the hot weather. I have always noticed with the guests who arrive at our monastery, how comforted they feel after a bowl of homemade soup is presented to them. It seems an anticipation of the warmth and peace they hope to find during their stay at the monastery.

The soups presented here follow the orderly cycle of the twelve months of the year, with emphasis on produce that is fresh and seasonal and thus available during that specific time of year. This repertoire offers a generous selection of soups per month for those who love to cook and eat a variety of soups, and it will encourage them to continue expanding their experience in the art of soup making.

The soups in this collection range from basic veloutés and consommés to thick and chunky soups, from simple clear broths to creamy soups and more complex potages. I have deliberately simplified the steps in every recipe to the bare essentials (as I do in all my books), so that anyone can easily try them. Throughout the years, many people have told me how they have been discouraged from trying new recipes after encountering so many long and complicated ones.

The recipes contained in this book are meant to help cultivate the art of soup making as well as provide appetizing and nutritious meals. About 75 percent of the recipes are vegetarian, and the rest of them can be easily adapted by vegetarians — for instance, by substituting vegetable stock or bouillon in place of its meat counterpart, or by eliminating the meat or the meat bones in the few places that call for it. Many of these recipes have been created and "re-created" in the kitchen of the monastery of Our Lady of the Resurrection in upstate New York. They are inspired by the simplicity, frugality, and family spirit of the monastic tradition, and they should be enjoyed in the intimacy of the family table. These recipes have nourished, comforted, and satisfied many throughout the years, and they can appeal to the most simple as well as the most refined of palates.

Soup making is an art to be discovered again and again; recipes are to be experimented with, tasted, and then enjoyed. Soup making is basic to life, and thus it is intimately linked to daily living with all that that implies: the rhythm of work and everyday routine, the change of seasons, the size and tastes of families, time limitations, the quality of ordinary meals as well as that of festive celebrations. Soups easily adapt themselves to any situation or circumstance of daily living, and often they bring much comfort to it. As someone once said, soup remains a faithful friend during all of life's occasions. Enjoy, then, the preparation of soups, and extend this joy to your family and friends by sharing the results with them in a warm spirit of conviviality and hospitality. As they say in France, invite them often *à la soupe.*

As we honor and pay tribute to soup, I also wish to encourage my readers to use the art of soup making to bring relief to the poor and the hungry near or around us. In ancient times, when monasteries were located within the city walls, monks and nuns provided soup and bread to the poor who daily knocked at their doors. Many monasteries still follow this ancient evangelical practice, and this is where the idea of "soup kitchens" to help the poor originated. Places like the Catholic Worker houses in New York City and other American cities daily alleviate the pangs of the hungry and comfort the poor and the weary with a bowl of homemade soup; these soup kitchens rely on the help of volunteers to fulfill their merciful task. Soup making, soup sharing, and soup giving done with love and a selfless spirit can be occasions for endless joy. As the Lord reminds us, whatever we do for the humblest members of his family, we do for him.

Before I put an end to these introductory notes, I wish to thank a long list of people who helped me along the way in the production of this book. First of all, I thank my parents and grandparents, and the many monks who preceded me in the kitchen and from whom I slowly learned the art of soup making. An early and good introduction to this art, as I look back, was very important in the process. Also, many thanks to my agent Howard Sandum, and my editors at Triumph Books, Joan Marlow Golan and Patricia Kossmann, for their encouragement and support. Thanks are also due and given here to the many friends who assisted me in the typing of this manuscript: Anne Poelzl, Eleanor Moorhouse, Jonathan Henry, and Sister J. Regis Catherwood, R.S.H.M., who patiently spent many hours with my scribbles. May the Lord remember them in his kingdom for all their goodness and service provided these past years.

I hope for many years to come you will enjoy with your friends and families the satisfaction that comes from making and sharing soup.

Brother Victor-Antoine d'Avila-Latourrette
January 17, 1996
Feast of our father among the saints,
Saint Antony the Great

Ingredients and Substitutions

The recipes presented here have a kind of universal character, since they spring from many sources and from the four corners of the world. The recipes are purposely written with great simplicity, so that anyone — not just professional cooks — will be encouraged to try them, and thus discover the joys and comforts of making, tasting, and eating soup.

To be truly enjoyed, a good soup needs to be served hot when the recipe calls for hot soup (whenever possible, always serve the hot soups in hot bowls) and cold when the recipe calls for cold soup.

Broth, Stock, and Bouillon

Broth — also called stock — is the basis for most soups, and they are so much better and richer if the broth or stock is homemade. Not all recipes call for a broth, and in some cases the soups create their own broth as they cook. In the Appendix of this book, I present recipes for the basic broths: meat, vegetable, chicken, and fish. Broth or stock is very simple to make, but it does take time. When the cook is in a hurry and isn't able to prepare the broth ahead of time, it is perfectly acceptable to use bouillon cubes or canned broth or consommé available from the supermarket. I bring bouillon cubes from France and use them frequently. However, the reader should be aware that American bouillon cubes and canned broths are quite

salty, and thus not advisable for those on low-sodium diets. When using bouillon cubes, you might want to omit adding any additional salt for taste.

Some of the recipes here specify a particular flavor of bouillon, which should be respected to give the soup the authentic taste of that recipe. Many other recipes use the generic term "bouillon" in the list of ingredients, and where no flavor is specified, you can choose the flavor of your preference. (Of course, vegetarians can and may always choose vegetable bouillon and achieve great satisfaction in their soups.) Please feel free to experiment with all kinds of bouillon until you discover the one you like best.

Vegetable Broth

A very convenient way to prepare a vegetable broth is to save the water in which vegetables are boiled. Keep saving and adding daily the boiled water from the vegetables you prepare in the course of a week to a container in the refrigerator, and you will have a basic vegetable stock, ready to be used and full of nutrients.

Simmering

"Simmering" is one of the most common words used in soup making. It is an integral part of the process and should not be taken lightly. Simmering has been defined as the quiet, languid movement of the liquids in the soup, which stays at a steady temperature while cooking. The purpose and reason for simmering the soup — that is, cooking it gently and for a long time — is to extract all the best flavors from the ingredients.

Cream Soups and Garnishes

A great number of soups can be made fat free. Cream soups, however, may require for their creaminess the use of milk, heavy cream, yogurt, or sour cream. In most of the recipes here, you can substitute low-fat or skim milk for regular milk, and nonfat yogurt and nonfat sour cream for the regular ones. In some cases, the soup requires heavy cream, and a substitution cannot be made without changing the nature and quality of the soup. In such cases, keep in mind that the fat will be shared by all, and each partaker of the soup will consume only a small amount of fat. If a particular cream soup requires a large number of eggs — say, four — and you are concerned about extra fat and cholesterol, you can cut the number of eggs in half to two, and the soup will still taste fine though less rich. Sour cream may be substituted for crème fraîche as a garnish.

Fat

Most soups require the use of some fat, either oil or butter, in their preparation. In recipes where no particular oil is specified, you can choose your preference. Many cooks, including myself, almost always use olive oil, which is the healthiest, especially for the cholesterol-conscious. (Use extra-virgin olive oil if possible.) Certain regional recipes such as those from Tuscany, Provence, and Spain require olive oil

for the authentic flavor, and normally another oil should not be substituted. Similarly, butter gives a distinctive flavor, which is lost if a substitution of another fat is made. Nevertheless, margarine may be used for those who prefer it. Those on low-fat diets may reduce the amount of oil or fat by, say, one third.

Seasonings and Herbs

One of the wonderful things about homemade soups, in contrast to those bought from the supermarket, is that you have complete control over the ingredients that go into the soup, especially the freshness and quality of them. Because so many people, for health reasons, need to limit sodium intake, I recommend that salt be used sparingly. I don't use much salt in my soups, and I often substitute lemon juice and other spices for it. Keep in mind that those who wish more salt in their soups may add it at the table.

Whenever it is possible, fresh-ground pepper should be used according to taste in any recipe that calls for pepper.

Herbs and spices, like salt and pepper, should be used according to taste, and naturally fresh herbs have better flavor than dry ones, especially the dried herbs in the supermarket. Here at the monastery, we have a good herb garden that provides fresh herbs for our table during the growing season. During the cold winter months, we preserve some herb plants in the greenhouse: for example, bay leaf, thyme, rosemary, etc. Other herbs from the garden we dry at harvest time and use in dried form.

January

"I give for the month of
January,
Courtyards and hall where fires
flame and flare."

— Folgore de San Gimignano

Saint Basil Soup

Ingredients   *4–6 servings*

6 tablespoons oil of choice
1 large onion, sliced
$^1/_2$ pound mushrooms, sliced
2 celery stalks, sliced
2 carrots, sliced

2 quarts water
2 bouillon cubes of choice
salt and pepper to taste
chopped parsley

1. Wash and thinly slice the vegetables.

2. Pour the oil into a soup pot. Add the vegetables and sauté them slightly for 2 or 3 minutes, stirring constantly.

3. Add the water and bouillon cubes. Cook the soup slowly in a covered pot over low heat for 30 minutes. Add salt and pepper and the chopped parsley. Simmer the soup for 10 minutes and serve hot.

This soup is a Western monastic version of a soup that has come down to us from an Orthodox monastery of the Middle East — hence it is named for the great father of Eastern monasticism. Saint Basil the Great (c. 330–379) came from a family remarkable both for wealth and distinction and for holiness — his grandparents, parents, and several siblings were also canonized as saints. During a famine that occurred just before his consecration as bishop of Caesarea in 370, he organized a soup kitchen and personally helped to feed the hungry, as well as donating his inherited wealth to the poor. Saint Basil's Rule is still followed by most Greek Orthodox monks and nuns, and Saint Benedict acknowledged Basil's inspiration in his own Rule.

Chickpea Soup à la Provençale

Ingredients   *6 servings*

2 cups dried chickpeas
$1/2$ cup olive oil
4 leeks, white part only, thinly sliced
10 cups water
$1/2$ pound chopped spinach
4 garlic cloves, minced

4 tablespoons herbs Provençal
  (thyme, rosemary, oregano,
  marjoram, bay leaf)
salt and pepper to taste
1 teaspoon butter or margarine
fried croutons (See recipe p. 195)

1. Soak the chickpeas overnight. Rinse them in cold water.

2. Pour the oil into a soup pot, add the thinly sliced leeks, and sauté gently over medium heat for a few minutes. Add the water, chickpeas, spinach, garlic, herbs, and seasonings.

3. Bring the soup to a boil, then reduce the heat to low-medium. Cover the pot and cook the soup slowly until the chickpeas are tender (50–60 minutes). Simmer for 15 minutes more.

4. When the soup is done, blend in a blender or food mill. Pour the soup back into the pot and reheat it. Serve the soup in hot bowls. Add butter and a few fried croutons to the top of each serving.

Chickpeas, or pois chiches, *as they are called in France, have always been a favorite in the Provençal cuisine — or, for that matter, in the cuisine of Mediterranean Europe. The combined flavors of the chickpeas, spinach, and leeks create a marvelous blend. And, of course, the leguminous nature of the chickpea adds an exquisite texture to the soup. To give a true "Provençal" flavor to the soup, be generous in your use of Provençal herbs and use a high-quality extra-virgin olive oil.*

Mushroom Soup à la Marie-Louise

Ingredients   *4 servings*

2 celery stalks, including leaves   5 cups water (add more if needed)
2 carrots   1 bay leaf
8 ounces fresh mushrooms   1 bouillon cube
1 large onion   1 teaspoon dried thyme
8 tablespoons oil   salt and pepper to taste

1. Cut the celery, carrots, mushrooms, and onion into thin slices. Mince the onion.

2. Pour the oil into a soup pot and add the onion. Sauté the onion for 1 or 2 minutes, stirring continuously. Add the celery and carrots and continue to stir for another 2 minutes.

3. Pour the water into the pot. Add the mushrooms, bay leaf, bouillon cube, thyme, salt, and pepper. Bring the soup to a boil and then let it cook over low heat, covered, for about 40 minutes. Remove the bay leaf and serve the soup hot.

"Soup makes an excellent hot first course. It's simple to prepare and requires very little last-minute attention, yet I have found that it's always greatly appreciated and people think you've gone to a great deal more trouble than you have."
— Rose Elliot, *The Festive Vegetarian*, 1983

Caldo Verde

(Portuguese Cabbage Soup)

Ingredients   *6 servings*

$^1/_2$ cup olive oil   8 cups chicken stock or water
3 onions, chopped   1 cup white wine
6 potatoes, peeled and cubed   salt and pepper to taste
1 small cabbage, chopped

1. Pour the oil into a soup pot and sauté the onions lightly for up to about 5 minutes. Stir often.

2. Add the potatoes, cabbage, chicken stock, wine, salt, and pepper. Bring the soup to a boil, then lower the heat and cover the pot. Simmer the soup for about 1 hour. Then turn off the heat and let the soup rest for 10 minutes. Serve hot.

Artichoke and Potato Soup

Ingredients   *6 servings*

$^1/_3$ cup olive oil
2 small onions, chopped
2 garlic cloves, minced
2 cups dry white wine
6 potatoes, peeled and cubed
2 14-ounce jars artichoke hearts,
   drained and then chopped

2 tablespoons lemon juice
6 cups chicken broth (or vegetable)
1 bay leaf
salt and pepper to taste
finely chopped parsley as garnish

1. Pour the olive oil into a soup pot and add the onions. Sauté gently over low heat for 2 minutes. Add the garlic and continue sautéing for another minute. Add the wine, cover the pot, and cook over very low heat for 5 more minutes.

2. Add the potatoes, artichokes, and lemon juice. Stir well, cover the pot, and continue cooking over very low heat for another 5 minutes.

3. Add the broth, bay leaf, salt, and pepper. Bring the soup to a boil and stir from time to time. Let it boil for about 5 minutes, then reduce the heat, cover the pot, and simmer for 30 minutes. Remove the bay leaf and serve the soup hot. Garnish with chopped parsley on top of each serving.

Cream of Pea Soup

Ingredients   *4 servings*

5 cups water
1 cup dried split peas
1 onion, minced
1 carrot, minced
3 bouillon cubes
1 bay leaf
salt to taste

1 teaspoon sugar
4 sprigs finely chopped parsley
3 tablespoons oil of choice (or butter
  or margarine)
3 tablespoons flour
2 cups milk
2 egg yolks

1. Pour the water into a soup pot and add the peas, onion, and carrot. Cook, covered, for about 30 minutes over low-medium heat, stirring from time to time. Add the bouillon cubes, bay leaf, salt, sugar, and parsley. Continue cooking over low heat for another 15 minutes.

2. Remove the bay leaf. Mix the oil and flour, making a paste, and then blend this mixture into the soup. Add milk. Stirring continuously, bring the soup to the boiling point and then add the eggs, first mixed in a bowl with a little bit of the soup. Cook for 1 or 2 minutes, stirring constantly, without letting the soup get to the boiling point. Serve hot.

This recipe is but one version of the many varieties of pea soup. Though in my opinion the eggs enhance the taste and smoothness of the soup a great deal, they can be omitted by those who have a cholesterol problem.

Brussels Sprout Soup

1 pound Brussels sprouts
3 leeks
2 quarts water
2 bouillon cubes
4 tablespoons olive oil

3 tablespoons flour
salt and pepper to taste
2 egg yolks
6 slices French bread

1. Cut the Brussels sprouts into thin slices. Slice the leeks and cook them in 1 quart of water for about 5 minutes. Add the bouillon cubes, olive oil, and the other quart of water. Continue cooking for another 40 minutes.

2. In a deep bowl, mix well the flour and 4 tablespoons of soup broth, making a smooth paste. Add this paste to the soup. Add salt and pepper and continue cooking for another 5 minutes. Stir well.

3. Remove the soup from the heat. Beat the egg yolks in 6 spoonfuls of soup broth.

4. Place a slice of bread in the center of a soup bowl, add 1 teaspoon of the egg mixture on top of the bread, then pour several ladlefuls of the hot soup on top of this. Serve immediately.

This is a very basic recipe that comes to us from the European region encompassing Belgium and northern France, where Brussels sprouts are popular in the local cuisine. The combination of flavors of the leeks and the Brussels sprouts creates a wonderful mild blend that is memorable for days after the soup is tasted. This soup may be prepared exactly as shown in the above recipe, or it may be mixed in a blender with a cup of milk and presented at the table as a creamy potage. Both versions are delicious. The potage variant makes a lovely introductory course to an elegant dinner.

Orzo Soup

½ cup olive oil
4 shallots, chopped
1 garlic clove, minced
5 cups water or vegetable stock
2 cups dry white wine
1 bouquet garni (oregano, thyme, and bay leaf, tied together and removed before serving)

salt and pepper to taste
½ cup finely chopped mushrooms
1 cup fresh or frozen green peas
1 cup Orzo noodles
sprinkle dried marjoram (fresh if you have it) and grated Romano cheese as garnish

1. Pour the olive oil into a soup pot and gently sauté the shallots and garlic for 1 minute. Stir often.

2. Add the water, wine, bouquet garni, salt, and pepper, and bring the mixture to a boil. Lower the heat to moderate and add the mushrooms and peas. Cover the pot and cook the soup for 30 minutes.

3. At this point, add the orzo noodles, check the seasonings, and add more wine if necessary. Simmer the soup, covered, gently for 15 minutes, then remove the bouquet garni and serve the soup hot. Sprinkle marjoram and some Romano cheese on the top of each serving.

"Of soup and love, the first is best."
— Spanish Proverb

Saint Antony Soup

4 tablespoons oil of choice
1 cup barley
3 carrots, grated
2 leeks, sliced
1 bay leaf

$1/2$ cup fresh minced parsley or
   chervil
salt to taste
7 cups water
1 bouillon cube and some chopped
   mushrooms (optional)

1. Pour the oil into a soup pot and add the barley, stirring continuously for 1 minute. Immediately add the carrots, leeks, bay leaf, parsley, salt, and water.

2. Cook the soup over low to medium heat for about 45 minutes, or until the barley is tender. Add more water if necessary. For extra taste, add the bouillon and mushrooms. Serve hot.

Saint Antony of Egypt, called the Great (A.D. 251–356), is considered the father of all monks. He was enormously popular in medieval times as a healer of both men and animals. At age 18, he was so moved by Christ's counsel to "sell all you have, give to the poor, and come follow me" that he did just that. Retiring to the desert as a hermit, he dedicated his life to God in continual prayer, while supporting himself by gardening and mat making. Among the multitudes who consulted Antony for spiritual advice was the emperor Constantine.

Velouté à la Dubarry

(Cauliflower Velouté)

Ingredients   *4 servings*

1 pound cauliflower
2 leeks (white part only)
1 potato, peeled
7 cups water
4 tablespoons butter
3 tablespoons flour

salt and white pepper to taste
2 egg yolks
1 cup dry vermouth
2 tablespoons sour cream
pinch of nutmeg

1. Chop the cauliflower and leeks and dice the potato. Place them in a large pot. Add the water and cook slowly, covered, over low-medium heat for 30 minutes.

2. Melt the butter in a separate pot. Gradually add the flour, salt, and pepper and make a roux (thickener), while stirring vigorously. Add some of the broth from the soup and mix well.

3. Place some cooked cauliflower florettes aside, then blend the rest of the vegetable mix in a blender. Return the soup to a clean soup pot. Add the roux, stir, and continue cooking, uncovered, over very low heat, not allowing the soup to reach the boiling point.

4. In a deep bowl, beat the egg yolks. Add the vermouth and sour cream and mix thoroughly. Pour this mixture into the soup. Add the nutmeg and stir well. Check the seasonings. Reheat the soup for a few minutes if it is cold, but again, do not allow it to boil. Serve hot, with the reserved cauliflower on top as garnish.

Cotriade Bretonne

(Fish Soup from Brittany)

---

8 tablespoons olive oil
3 onions, chopped
6 garlic cloves, chopped and minced
10 cups water
bouquet garni (thyme, bay leaf,
    parsley, and chervil), tied together
    and removed before serving
8 potatoes, sliced in quarters

$^3/_4$ pound mackerel (or other fish),
    cleaned and cut in chunks
$^3/_4$ pound codfish (or other fish),
    cleaned and cut in chunks
salt and pepper to taste
1 cup white wine
6 tablespoons chives (or chervil),
    finely chopped
croutons (see recipe p. 195)

Vinaigrette:
$^1/_2$ cup olive oil
$^1/_4$ cup balsamic vinegar

salt and pepper to taste
a pinch of dry mustard

1. Pour the olive oil in a soup pot and sauté the onions lightly for 2 or 3 minutes. Add the garlic, water, and bouquet garni, and bring to a boil.

2. Add the potatoes, cover the pot, and cook gently for about 30 minutes. Add the fish, salt, pepper, and wine and continue cooking the soup, covered, at a light boil for 15 more minutes.

3. Remove the pot from the heat and pass the soup through a colander. Place the solid parts (fish and potatoes) aside. Ladle the soup bouillon into deep bowls, sprinkle some finely chopped chives on top, add the croutons as garnish, and serve hot.

4. Prepare the vinaigrette by mixing all the ingredients together. Place an equal amount of fish and potato on each plate. Pour the vinaigrette on top and serve immediately after the soup. You may use freshly chopped parsley or chervil as a garnish on top of the vinaigrette.

For a bit of extra taste, add one more cup of dry white wine to the bouillon.

Cherbah

(Arabic Soup)

Ingredients   *4–6 servings*

1/4 cup olive oil	1/2 cup finely chopped mint
3 onions, sliced	6 cups stock (vegetable or meat)
6 tomatoes, peeled and coarsely chopped	4 tablespoons lemon juice
3 garlic cloves, chopped	egg yolk, beaten
1 6-ounce jar red pimientos, chopped	6 bread slices
	salt and pepper to taste

1. Heat the olive oil in a soup pot. Add the onions, tomatoes, and garlic. Sauté for 3 minutes, stirring frequently.

2. Add the pimientos and mint and mix well. Immediately afterward, add the stock (or water and 3 bouillon cubes) and lemon juice and bring to a boil. Cover the soup, lower the heat to low-medium, and simmer for 30 minutes.

3. Add the seasonings and blend the beaten egg yolk with 4 tablespoons of the soup. Add this egg mixture to the soup and stir vigorously so it all blends well. Serve the soup hot over 1 slice of bread in the center of each serving.

Black-Eyed Pea Soup

1/4 cup olive oil
2 onions or leeks, chopped
1 turnip, diced
1 cup black-eyed peas (or 1 15-ounce can)
7 cups vegetable or chicken broth
2/3 cup rice

salt and pepper to taste
1 bay leaf
6 tablespoons lemon juice (or juice from 2 lemons)
pinch of cumin
1/3 cup fresh parsley, minced

1. Pour the oil into a soup pot and sauté the onions for 2 or 3 minutes, or until they turn golden.

2. Add the turnip, black-eyed peas, broth, rice, salt, pepper, and bay leaf and bring the soup to a boil. Reduce the heat to low-medium, cover the pot, and simmer the soup slowly for 45 minutes, or until the peas are cooked.

3. Add the lemon juice and cumin and stir the soup well. Allow it to sit, covered, for 5 minutes. Remove the bay leaf and serve hot. Sprinkle some fresh parsley on top of each serving.

Spicy English Parsnip Soup

4 parsnips, peeled and sliced
2 medium-sized potatoes, peeled and
  cubed
1 large onion, chopped
1 garlic clove, minced
4 tablespoons butter, margarine, or
  oil of choice

1 teaspoon curry powder
$1/2$ teaspoon ginger powder
6 cups stock of choice
$1/2$ cup half-and-half or heavy cream
salt and white pepper to taste
chopped parsley, as garnish

1. Melt the butter in a good-sized soup pot and add the prepared vegetables. Sauté them lightly for 2 to 3 minutes.

2. Sprinkle the curry and ginger on top and stir the vegetables thoroughly. Add the stock and bring the soup to a boil. Lower the heat and simmer the soup, covered, for 30 minutes.

3. Blend the soup in a blender or food processor until thick and creamy and then return it to the pot. Reheat the soup, add the half-and-half and the seasonings, and stir well. Add more curry if the soup seems to need it. Do not let the soup come to a second boil. Serve the soup hot with some finely chopped parsley as garnish.

The love and taste for parsnips is peculiar to the British Isles and is shared equally by the British and the Irish. Continental Europeans and their South American counterparts regard parsnips as food for cattle and pigs. They may occasionally be used in France in a stew, but rarely. In the United States, parsnips are often used in soups with other vegetables. I happen to like the individual flavor of parsnips, and I think this soup demonstrates the good use we can make of them.

Spinach Cream Soup

Ingredients

1 package fresh spinach (frozen may be substituted)

1 onion, sliced

4 tablespoons olive oil

7 cups chicken stock

3 eggs

6 tablespoons grated Parmesan cheese

salt, pepper, and nutmeg to taste

2 garlic cloves, minced

6 slices bread

1. Wash the spinach, making sure it is well cleaned. Then chop it. Chop the onion.

2. Pour the olive oil into a soup pot and briefly sauté the spinach and onion. After 3 minutes, add the chicken stock and cook slowly over low heat for about 30 minutes. Add more stock if necessary.

3. Beat the eggs and Parmesan cheese in a deep bowl. Add salt, pepper, and nutmeg and mix it all very well.

4. Blend the soup in a blender until thick and creamy and return it to the pot. Add the egg mixture and stir continually until all the elements blend well. Reheat the soup over low heat for about 5 to 8 minutes.

5. Rub the garlic on the slices of bread and place them in the oven for a few minutes. Place a bread slice in each bowl and immediately pour the hot soup on top. Serve hot.

February

"Come when the rains
Have glazed the snow and clothed the trees with ice,
while the slant sun of February pours
Into the bowers of a flood of light."

—William Cullen Bryant

Potage de Navets

(Turnip Soup)

Ingredients   *4 servings*

1 pound turnips
2 onions or shallots
1 cup rice
1 1/2 quarts water
2 cups milk (low-fat can be used)

1/2 cup heavy cream or half-and-half
2 tablespoons butter or margarine
salt and pepper to taste
croutons (optional; see recipe p. 195)

1. Slice the turnips in quarters. Place them in the soup pot, add the onions, rice, and water, and boil slowly in a covered pot until vegetables and rice are cooked. Stir from time to time.

2. Take the solid part from the soup, mash it, then put it back into the soup.

3. Add the milk, stirring constantly, while reheating to the boiling point. Add the cream, butter, salt, and pepper and continue stirring for another minute or so. Serve hot. Add a few croutons to each serving as garnish.

"The turnip deserves better treatment than it gets in most kitchens. It is one of our oldest vegetables, cultivated by man for its edible leaves and root for more than 4,000 years. It is popular in France, where it is often part of elegant dishes and cooked in many inventive fashions, yet its versatility is little known or appreciated in the U.S."
—Bernard Clayton, Jr., *The Complete Book of Soups and Stews*

Saint Scholastica Soup

(Soupe Sainte Scholastique)

Ingredients   *4 servings*

3 quarts water (more if needed)
10 tablespoons lentils
10 tablespoons split peas
8 tablespoons lima beans
2 leeks, finely chopped
4 shallots, finely chopped

2 long carrots, finely chopped
2 medium turnips, finely chopped
1 celery stalk, finely chopped
1 small head lettuce, finely chopped
3 ounces butter or margarine
salt and pepper to taste

1. Pour water into large soup pot. Add the lentils, split peas, and beans and bring to a boil.

2. Add the leeks, shallots, carrots, turnips, and celery stalk. Continue boiling over medium heat in a covered pot for about 30 minutes. Then add the lettuce and simmer for another 30 minutes over a very low heat.

3. Add the butter, salt, and pepper and stir well. Let soup sit, covered, for about 10 to 15 minutes. Serve hot.

Saint Scholastica (d. c. 543) was Saint Benedict's twin, and she was one of the first women to embrace monastic life under the Rule written by her brother. Once a year, she and her brother met halfway between their respective monasteries. On their last visit, after Benedict had resisted his sister's urging to stay and prolong their discussion of the joys of heaven, she prayed for rain to detain him and was answered with a violent thunderstorm. The feast of this revered mother of nuns is celebrated on February 10, and is one of those lovely monastic feasts that brighten our long, dark winters.

French Lentil Soup

6 tablespoons olive oil
1 large onion, chopped
2 garlic cloves, minced
1 1/2 cups lentils
3 quarts water (more if needed)
1 celery stalk, cut fine
1 turnip, diced

1 bunch sorrel or spinach leaves
1 bay leaf
1 large carrot, finely cut
1 large potato, diced
1 cup tomato sauce
salt and pepper to taste
1/2 cup cooked rice (optional)

1. Pour the olive oil into the soup pot and gently sauté the onion and garlic for 2 minutes. Stir continually.

2. Wash and rinse the lentils and add them to the soup pot. Add the water, cut vegetables, and the rest of the ingredients except the salt and pepper and rice. Bring to a boil. Then lower the heat to medium and cook slowly, covered, for 1 hour.

3. Add the salt and pepper and let the soup simmer a short while longer. Remove the bay leaf. Serve hot. Add cooked rice if desired.

There are endless varieties of lentil soups. This particular recipe comes to us from France, where two varieties of lentils are grown that can be used for this soup (either the green ones or the dark brown ones). These French lentils are a bit smaller and a bit crunchier than the lentils sold in American supermarkets. This recipe suggests adding rice for the simple reason that the combination of rice and lentils produces the complete protein needed in the daily diet.

Garlic Royale

2 quarts water (more if needed)
4 bouillon cubes (or chicken stock instead of bouillon and water)
10 garlic cloves, minced
1 cup white wine
1 bouquet garni (thyme, bay leaf, parsley, tied together in cheesecloth)

salt and pepper to taste
dash Tabasco
2 egg yolks beaten
$^1/_2$ cup heavy cream

1. Bring the water to a boil. Add the garlic, bouillon cubes, wine, and bouquet garni. Cover the pot and cook slowly for over 1 hour. Add more water if necessary.

2. Strain the consommé through a thin colander and discard all the solids. Place the consommé back into the pot and add salt, pepper, and Tabasco. Bring to a boil and let the soup simmer for 10 minutes.

3. Just before serving, beat the egg yolks and heavy cream. Pour this mixture into the consommé and stir well. Serve immediately.

  "Surely one of the greatest satisfactions of life is to cook a really delicious meal, a meal that nourishes the body and cheers the spirit, and may be remembered with pleasure for a long time to come."
—Rose Elliot, *The Festive Vegetarian*

Polish Pearl Barley Soup

4 tablespoons vegetable oil
3 leeks, chopped
2 carrots, peeled and sliced
1 celery heart, chopped
1 turnip, diced

8 cups meat broth (or vegetable)
1 cup barley
salt and pepper to taste
$^1\!/_3$ cup parsley, chopped
sour cream

1. Pour the oil into the saucepan and gently sauté the leeks, carrots, celery, and turnip for about 3 minutes. Stir often.

2. Add the broth, barley, salt, and pepper and bring the soup to a boil. Lower the heat, cover the pot, and simmer the soup slowly for 45 to 50 minutes. Add the parsley, stir well, and turn off the heat. Cover the pot and let the soup rest for 10 minutes.

3. Serve the soup hot and place 1 teaspoon sour cream at the center of each serving.

Quick Black Bean Mexican Soup

$^1/_3$ cup olive oil
1 large yellow onion, chopped
4 garlic cloves, minced
1 jalapeño pepper, chopped finely
2 tomatoes, peeled and chopped
2 15-ounce cans black beans
2 potatoes, peeled and diced
7 cups water

1 bouillon cube
$^1/_2$ cup fresh cilantro, chopped
1 tablespoon cumin
2 tablespoons lime juice
salt and pepper to taste
sour cream as garnish with freshly
   chopped cilantro all around

1. Pour the olive oil into a good-sized soup pot and sauté the onion for 2 minutes. Add the garlic, jalapeño pepper, and tomatoes, and continue sautéing for another 2 minutes over medium heat, until it turns into a regular sauce. Stir often.

2. Add the beans from their cans with their juice, potatoes, water, and bouillon. Bring the soup to a boil and then reduce the heat to low-medium. Cook slowly, covered, for about 20 minutes.

3. Add the cilantro, cumin, lime juice, salt, and pepper. Stir well and continue cooking for another 10 minutes, turn off the heat, and let the soup rest, covered, for 5 minutes. Serve hot and garnish each serving with a teaspoon of sour cream in the center and freshly chopped cilantro around the sour cream.

This is one variation among many traditional Mexican black bean soups. It is a particularly hearty soup with a distinctive flavor of its own because of the jalapeño pepper, cumin, lime juice, and cilantro, which are popular spices in Mexican cooking. The sharp, hot flavor of the jalapeño pepper can be reduced by using only half of it, or even omitting it altogether. The garnishes, on the other hand, are very important for the success of this soup, and I recommend strongly that they not be omitted.

Escarole and Bean Minestra

Ingredients

8 tablespoons olive oil
1 large yellow onion, chopped
6 garlic cloves, minced
1 large turnip, diced
4 tomatoes, peeled and chopped
2 cups precooked white beans or 2
  16-ounce cans of the same beans

7 cups water
1 cup white wine
1 medium-sized head escarole,
  chopped
salt and pepper to taste
grated Parmesan cheese (optional)

1. In a large soup pot, sauté the onion in the oil for a minute or two. Add the minced garlic and mix it well with the onion, stirring often. Add the turnip and tomatoes. Cook the soup over medium heat for 5 minutes, stirring often.

2. Add the precooked beans, water, and wine. Stir the soup and bring it to a boil. Add the escarole and cook the soup over medium heat for about 25 minutes. Add the salt and pepper and simmer for another 10 minutes. Serve hot. You may sprinkle some grated cheese on top.

The slightly bitter-sour flavor of escarole is always welcome, especially as the main ingredient in a traditional Italian soup. Escarole, like many other greens, is extremely rich in vitamins and minerals, and it is readily available in supermarkets all year round. In this particular recipe, the escarole is combined with white beans, producing a wonderfully rich, flavorful soup. For a bit of extra taste, add a bouillon cube — chicken flavor or flavor of choice. One cup of dry white wine also enhances the flavor of the soup.

Old-fashioned Cream of Leek Provençal Soup

Ingredients *6—8 servings*

½ cup olive oil
12 leeks (white part only), chopped
8 cups water
3 cups day-old bread (more if
    needed)

3 egg yolks (or at least 2)
2 cups milk
salt and pepper to taste
croutons as garnish (see recipe
    p. 195)

---

1. Sauté the chopped leeks in the oil in a large soup pot over low heat for a few minutes, stirring frequently. (Do not let the leeks turn golden or change color.) Add the water immediately and bring to a boil.

2. Add the day-old bread. Cover and simmer the soup for 30 minutes, until the leeks are well cooked. Season with salt and pepper. Pass the soup through a sieve or blend in blender. Return the soup to the pot and keep it hot.

3. Break the eggs into a bowl and beat them. Add the milk, salt, and pepper, and blend thoroughly. Add this mixture to the soup, reheat and blend well, and serve it while the soup is hot. Add the croutons on top as garnish.

Bouillabaisse à la Marseillaise

1/3 cup olive oil
2 onions, chopped and minced
4 garlic cloves, minced
3 tomatoes, peeled, seeded, and
   chopped
1 fennel bulb, finely chopped
6 parsley sprigs, finely chopped
salt and pepper to taste
8 cups water
1 bay leaf
3 potatoes, peeled and diced
8 large shrimps
8 scallops or mussels (discard shells)
1/2 pound haddock, cod, halibut,
   monkfish, or rockfish, cleaned and
   cut in small pieces

1 cup dry white wine
a good pinch saffron

Sauce Rouille (optional)
4 garlic cloves, peeled and crushed
2 egg yolks
1 tablespoon lemon juice (or dry
   white wine)
1 tablespoon Dijon mustard
salt and paprika to taste
1 1/2 cups olive oil

1. Heat the oil in a good-sized soup pot. Add the onions, garlic, tomatoes, and fennel. Sauté them lightly over low heat for 2 or 3 minutes.

2. Add the parsley, salt, pepper, water, and bay leaf and bring the soup to a light boil. Simmer the soup for a few minutes, then add the potatoes, scallops, shrimp, cut fish, saffron, and wine. Stir well.

3. Cover the pot and cook the bouillabaisse over high heat for 15 minutes. Then reduce the heat and simmer the soup for another 15 minutes.

4. To make the Rouille or aioli (garlic) sauce, combine all ingredients except the oil in a deep bowl. Mix slowly with an electric mixer. Then, one drop at a time, add the oil until the Rouille thickens to the consistency of mayonnaise. Refrigerate before serving.

5. Ladle into soup bowls as is, or separate the potatoes and the fish, remove the bay leaf, and serve only the broth over slices of French bread covered with a Rouille spread. In that case, serve the potatoes and the fish afterward in a separate dish with more Rouille sauce on the side.

"This bouillabaisse a noble dish
is —
A sort of soup, or broth, or brew,
Or hotchpotch of all sorts of
fishes,
That Greenwich never could outdo;
Green herbs, red peppers, mussels, saffron,
Sole, onions, garlic, roach, and dace;
All of these you eat at Terre's tavern
In that one dish Bouillabaisse."

—William Makepeace Thackeray,
Ballad of Bouillabaisse

Country Mushroom and Sour Cream Soup

Ingredients

1 pound fresh mushrooms, finely chopped

1 large carrot, cut julienne style

1 potato, diced

2 large onions, finely sliced

8 tablespoons olive oil

6 cups water (more if needed)

1 bouillon cube

salt and paprika to taste

1 cup sour cream

chopped chives as garnish

1. Prepare the vegetables. Place the oil in a soup pot. Sauté the mushrooms, carrot, potato, and onions for 3 to 4 minutes, stirring continually.

2. Add the water and bouillon cube and cook slowly, covered, over medium heat for 30 to 40 minutes. Add the salt, paprika, and the cup of sour cream. Stir and mix well and simmer for 10 minutes. Serve the soup hot, sprinkling some finely chopped chives on top as garnish.

This is a delicious creamy soup, lavishly enhanced by the thin slices of fresh mushrooms. (Never substitute canned mushrooms for fresh mushrooms, especially in soup, or you will sacrifice flavor and texture.) The sour cream adds an unexpected and inspired touch. This soup must always be served hot.

Soupe du Berry

(Red Bean Soup from Berry)

Ingredients   *6 servings*

$^1/_2$ cup olive oil   4 cups water or vegetable stock

3 onions, chopped   1 ham bone

3 cups precooked red beans or the   1 bay leaf

   equivalent in canned red beans   salt and pepper to taste

1 bottle red wine $^1/_4$ teaspoon nutmeg

1. Pour the olive oil into the soup pot and add the onions. Sauté for 2 to 3 minutes. Add the red beans, wine, water, ham bone, and bay leaf. Bring the soup to a boil. Then lower the heat to medium-low, cover the pot, and let the soup simmer for 1 hour.

2. Add salt, pepper, and nutmeg. Stir well and continue cooking for another 15 minutes. Turn off the heat and let the soup rest for 10 minutes. Remove the bay leaf and ham bone and serve the soup hot.

Ravioli Potage

¹/₃ cup olive oil

2 shallots, chopped

3 tomatoes, peeled, seeded, and
  chopped

1 ¹/₂ cups chopped spinach

5 cups chicken stock (or water and 2
  bouillon cubes)

20 ounces fresh or frozen small
  ravioli

salt and pepper to taste

4 sprigs of chervil, chopped

4 teaspoons crème fraîche or sour
  cream, as garnish

1. Pour the oil into a good-sized soup pot. Add the shallots and tomatoes. Sauté them gently for
   3 minutes.

2. Add the spinach and the stock. Stir and slowly bring the soup to a boil. Simmer for about 15
   minutes.

3. Add the ravioli, salt, and pepper. Cover the pot and continue simmering for about 8 minutes.
   Add the chervil, stir, and cover the pot. Turn off the heat and let the soup rest for 5 minutes.
   Serve the soup hot, and place 1 teaspoon crème fraîche in the center of each of the soup bowls.

Cheese Velouté

Ingredients *4 servings*

5 cups chicken stock or bouillon
10 tablespoons tapioca
3 egg yolks
1 pint heavy cream or half-and-half

²/₃ cup grated Gruyère or Parmesan
  cheese
salt and pepper to taste
chervil, finely chopped, as garnish

1. Heat the stock and gently bring it to a boil. Sprinkle the tapioca gradually into the boiling stock and stir very well. Cook over low-medium heat for about 20 minutes.

2. Place the egg yolks and cream into a deep bowl and mix thoroughly with an electric mixer. Add the cheese slowly and continue to mix to obtain a smooth mixture.

3. Slowly pour the egg-cream mixture into the hot stock. Add salt and pepper. Stir continually and mix very well. Serve the soup hot, sprinkling some finely chopped chervil on top of each serving.

Bulgarian Soup

Ingredients

2 quarts beef broth	2 tablespoons butter or margarine
4 carrots, diced	1 teaspoon flour
3 white turnips, diced	salt and pepper to taste
1 small celeriac, diced	2 eggs
1 cup rice	4 tablespoons lemon juice
1 large onion	chopped parsley

1. Pour the broth into a large soup pot. Add all the vegetables and rice and cook slowly over medium heat with the pot covered for about 30 minutes.

2. Peel and slice the onion. Melt the butter and sauté the onion briefly, until it begins to turn. Add the flour and mix thoroughly until even.

3. Add the onion mixture and salt and pepper to the soup and continue cooking for 10 minutes.

4. Just before serving, beat the eggs thoroughly with the lemon juice. Add to the soup and stir continually for 1 minute. Serve the soup hot, garnished with finely chopped parsley.

March

"White peason, both good for the pot and the purse,
by sowing too timely, prove often the worse;
Because they be tender, and hateth the cold,
prove March ere ye sow them, for being too bold."

—Thomas Tusser

Saint Lioba Beer and Mushroom Soup

Ingredients *4–6 servings*

6 tablespoons oil of choice
2 cups mushrooms, chopped
2 large onions, chopped
6 cans beer
1 bay leaf

2 eggs
4 tablespoons heavy cream
chopped parsley
salt and pepper to taste
grated Gruyère cheese

1. Pour the oil into a soup pot. Add the mushrooms and onions. Sauté them lightly for a few minutes over low heat. Add the beer and bay leaf and raise the heat to medium. Bring the soup to a boil, then simmer slowly for about 20 minutes.

2. In the meantime, in a bowl beat and blend well the eggs and cream. Add 6 tablespoons hot soup to the egg mixture and blend thoroughly.

3. Pour the mixture into the soup, mixing well. Add the chopped parsley, salt, and pepper, and mix well. Reheat the soup over medium heat and continue stirring for a few minutes. Remove the bay leaf and serve the soup hot. Sprinkle some grated cheese on top of each serving.

This German soup is named after Saint Lioba (d. 782), who played a pivotal role in the evangelization of Germany. An Englishwoman, she founded a monastery of nuns in Germany at the request of her cousin Saint Boniface, who later requested she be buried near him. Her monastery became a center of Christian culture from which abbesses for other houses were taken. Saint Lioba's name means "dear one," and her beauty, intelligence, patience, and loving-kindness endeared her to all who knew her.

Spicy Indian Soup

⅓ cup olive oil	1 teaspoon ground coriander
2 onions, chopped	1 teaspoon cumin
2 garlic cloves, minced	½ teaspoon curry powder
2½ cups brown or green lentils	½ teaspoon paprika
8 cups water	6 tablespoons lemon juice
2 carrots, peeled and finely sliced	2 teaspoons grated lemon peel
2 celery sticks, finely sliced	salt and pepper to taste

1. Pour the oil into a large soup pot. Add the onions, garlic, and lentils. Sauté gently over low heat for about 3 minutes. Stir continually and watch that the vegetables don't stick at the bottom of the pot.

2. Pour the water into the mixture, stir, and raise the heat to medium. Bring the soup to a boil and add the carrots and celery. Boil for about 20 minutes and then lower the heat to low-medium.

3. Add the coriander, cumin, curry, paprika, lemon juice, lemon peel, salt, and pepper. Stir well and cover the pot. Let the soup simmer gently for about 45 minutes. Check the seasonings and serve hot.

Basic Onion Soup

Ingredients   *6 servings*

6 large onions
6 tablespoons olive oil
6 cups water or stock of choice
4 bouillon cubes (if soup stock is not
   used)

6 slices bread, toasted
salt and pepper to taste
grated Gruyère cheese

1. Cut the onion into thin slices. Pour the oil into the soup pot and cook the onions slowly until they turn brown. Stir continually.

2. Add the water and bouillon cubes. Bring the water to a boil, boil for 5 minutes, and simmer for 10 more. Add the salt and pepper. Stir well.

3. Pour the soup into oven-proof soup bowls. Add a slice of toasted bread on top, cover the entire top of the bowls with grated cheese, and carefully place the bowls into a preheated oven (350°) for 5 to 10 minutes. Serve the soup when the cheese begins to bubble.

French onion soup is probably one of the most popular soups in the world, and there are endless recipes on how to prepare it. The version provided here is one of the easiest. The soup tastes infinitely better with a rich homemade beef or vegetable stock instead of the bouillon cubes. This particular recipe has been reduced to extreme simplicity for the sake of those who lack time to prepare an elaborate soup. For extra flavor and tonic, add to the soup a pinch of cayenne and 4 tablespoons of Calvados liqueur.

Minestrone di Verdura

(Tuscan Green Vegetable Minestrone)

Ingredients   *6–8 servings*

²/₃ cup olive oil
large onion, chopped
2 carrots, sliced
2 celery stalks, sliced
1 15-ounce can cooked cannellini
  beans
1 15-ounce can peeled tomatoes

10 cups water
2 potatoes, peeled and diced
small radicchio, chopped
1 cup white wine
1 bay leaf
chopped parsley
salt and pepper to taste

1. Gently sauté in olive oil the onion, carrots, and celery stalks for about 5 minutes. Add the beans and tomatoes and continue sautéing for 2 more minutes.

2. Add water and bring the soup to a boil. Add the diced potatoes, radicchio, wine, bay leaf, parsley, salt, and pepper. Cover the pot and simmer the soup for 60 minutes. Turn off the heat and let the soup stand for 15 minutes. Remove the bay leaf. Serve hot. Grated cheese may be sprinkled on top of each serving.

Everyday Potato Soup

Ingredients   *6 servings*

8 potatoes, peeled and diced
2 quarts water or stock of choice
3 onions, sliced
1 cup milk

salt and pepper to taste
2 tablespoons butter or oil of choice
4 teaspoons chopped parsley (or chervil)

1. Put the potatoes into a soup pot. Add the water and onions and cook over low-medium heat, covered, for about 45 minutes.

2. With a hand masher, mash the potatoes in the soup pot. Add the milk, salt, and pepper and stir the soup, then reheat.

3. Just before serving, add the butter and parsley. Stir and mix well. Serve hot during the cold weather and cold during the warm weather. (When soup is served cold, oil must be used instead of butter.)

This is an easy and economical soup to prepare because all that is needed are some potatoes, a few onions, and a cup of milk. To enhance the soup a bit, add plenty of tender finely chopped fresh parsley. The garnish is a must for a simple soup such as this one.

Garlic Soup

10 large cloves of garlic, well minced
$1/2$ cup olive oil
7 cups water or stock of choice
3 bouillon cubes if stock not used
1 15-ounce can of tomato sauce

8 slices French bread
1 bay leaf
salt and pepper to taste
2 well-beaten eggs
pinch of cayenne (optional)

1. Sauté garlic in olive oil over low heat without allowing it to brown or burn. Stir continually. Add 3 cups water, bouillon cubes, and tomato sauce. Stir well.

2. Blend the soup in a blender until smooth. Return it to the pot and add remaining water, French bread, bay leaf, salt, and pepper. Bring to a boil, stirring continually, then reduce heat and let cook for about 15 minutes. Then simmer slowly for another 15 minutes. Add cayenne and remove bay leaf.

3. In a deep bowl, beat the 2 eggs gently, adding half a cup of the soup to them and blending the mixture very well. Pour this mixture slowly into the soup, stirring constantly. Simmer for another 5 minutes. Serve hot.

This is a delicious and aromatic soup that is perfectly suited for a cold day in winter. As presented in this recipe, the soup is a popular dish in southern France and northern Spain, where the love of garlic is legendary. Though in the recipe I recommend the use of a blender, a mortar can be use to crush the garlic, as the people of France and Spain still do to this day. And if the tomato sauce (made at home, I hope) remains thick and coarse, so much the better, for it will add texture to the soup.

Lima Bean Soup

4 tablespoons olive oil
1 onion, chopped
3 garlic cloves, minced
7 cups water
1 carrot, sliced
2 potatoes, sliced in cubes
1 bouillon cube

2 cups fresh, dried, or frozen lima
  beans
parsley, chopped
salt and pepper to taste
grated cheese of choice as garnish
  (optional)

1. Pour the oil into a good-sized soup pot. Add the onion and the garlic and sauté lightly for a minute or two over low heat. Stir continually.

2. Add the water, carrot, potatoes, and bouillon cube. Bring to a boil over medium heat and then reduce the heat to low.

3. Add the lima beans (less with frozen beans), chopped parsley, salt, and pepper. Cook slowly, over low-medium heat, for about 1 hour, or until the beans are tender. Let the soup sit for 5 minutes, and then serve it hot. Some grated cheese may be sprinkled as garnish on top of each serving.

Béguine Cream Soup

Ingredients *4–6 servings*

7 cups water
2 leeks
4 large potatoes, peeled and diced
4 carrots, peeled and sliced
4 slices stale bread

salt and pepper to taste
$1/2$ teaspoon nutmeg
1 cup half-and-half
1 tablespoon butter or margarine
chopped parsley and chopped chervil

1. Bring water to a boil in a large soup pot. Add the leeks, potatoes, carrots, and bread slices. Lower the heat to moderate, cover the pot, and cook for about 1 hour.

2. Add salt and pepper to taste. Stir the soup. Turn off the soup and let it rest for 5 minutes. Then blend the soup in a food mill or blender till thick and creamy.

3. Return the soup to the pot. Add the nutmeg, half-and-half, and butter. Stir well and bring to a light boil. Add chopped parsley and chervil and serve at once.

This recipe is the version of a soup from Flanders in northern Belgium. Its name suggests it originated among the Béguines. Béguinage was a medieval institution that allowed pious laywomen to lead a form of religious life in common, without becoming actual nuns. It was one of the few alternatives to either marriage or the cloister. The Béguines lived in beautiful small houses attached to each other. They were independent and were allowed to keep their servants. However, they had a common church for their devotions, and they had each other for mutual company. In general, they were a progressive group of women who wished to assert, as much as the times allowed, their independence from men. They were women of great culture, and some of them became renowned mystics. The Béguines, as an institution, flourished particularly in Holland and the Flemish section of Belgium.

Bread and Milk Soup

Ingredients   *4 servings*

4 tablespoons butter or margarine   4 slices bread cut into quarters
4 tablespoons flour   salt and pepper to taste
1 quart milk (more if necessary)   1 beaten egg
1 onion, chopped and minced $1/2$ cup chopped parsley or chervil

1. Melt the butter in a soup pot. Add the flour and half a cup of milk, stirring all the time.

2. Add the onion and the rest of the milk. Bring the soup to a boil. Add the bread and seasonings and simmer the soup for 10 to 15 minutes. Stir occasionally.

3. When the soup is done, add the beaten egg and blend thoroughly. Sprinkle the fresh chopped parsley on top of the soup. Serve hot.

"Soup as a main course,
soup to begin the meal,
— and when it is homemade,
it is soup to nourish the soul."
—Julia Child, *The French Chef Cookbook*

Fava Bean Soup

2 onions, chopped fine
$^1/_3$ cup olive oil
1 16-ounce can fava beans (or the
    equivalent in dried ones soaked
    overnight and rinsed twice in
    fresh water)
1 carrot, diced
1 large potato, peeled and diced
6 cups water

1 cup fresh or frozen peas
1 small branch thyme (or 1 teaspoon
    dried thyme)
1 ham bone (or 1 slice ham thinly
    cut)
$^1/_3$ cup sherry
salt and cayenne pepper to taste
croutons (optional; see recipe p. 195)

1. Place the onions in the soup pot and sauté them in olive oil for about 2 minutes. Stir frequently.

2. Add the fava beans (without their juice), carrot, and potato. Stir well and add the water. Over medium heat, bring the water to a boil.

3. When the water is boiling, add the peas, thyme, and ham bone and cover the pot. Cook slowly over low-medium heat for 30 minutes.

4. Add the sherry, salt, and cayenne pepper (just a dash). Stir well, cover the pot, and simmer for another 15 minutes. Remove the ham bone and the thyme. Add the croutons on top of each serving as garnish.

Watercress Soup

Ingredients   *4–6 servings*

4 tablespoons butter, margarine, or
   oil of choice

4 leeks, chopped

1 bunch fresh watercress, chopped

4 potatoes, peeled and cubed

5 cups water (or stock of choice)

1 bouillon cube (if water is used
   instead of stock)

1 ½ cups milk (for richer soup, use
   1 cup cream instead)

salt and pepper to taste

1 egg yolk, beaten (optional)

6 tablespoons crème fraîche, as
   garnish

chopped chervil, as garnish

1. Melt the butter or oil in a large soup pot. Add the leeks and watercress and sauté them gently for 2 to 3 minutes.

2. Add the potatoes and continue sautéing for 1 minute extra, stirring frequently. Add the water or stock and the bouillon cube (if necessary). Bring the soup to a boil, and then cover the pot. Simmer the soup gently for 30 minutes.

3. Blend the soup in a blender and return it to the pot. Add milk and simmer for another 10 minutes. (At this point, if you wish, add the egg yolk and mix thoroughly).

4. Serve the soup in well-heated bowls. Place 1 teaspoon of crème fraîche in the center of each serving and sprinkle the chopped chervil all around it.

Saint Patrick Irish Cheddar Soup

Ingredients   *4–6 servings*

2 leeks   ¼ teaspoon sage powder
2 potatoes   salt and pepper to taste
4 carrots   1 cup milk
4 tablespoons butter or margarine   5 ounces grated Kerrygold Irish
6 cups vegetable or meat stock   Cheddar cheese (or any mild
1 garlic clove, minced   cheddar
¼ teaspoon thyme powder

1. Clean, peel, and chop the vegetables. Melt the butter in a soup pot and sauté the vegetables lightly for about 3 minutes. Stir frequently.

2. Add the stock, garlic, herbs, and seasonings. Bring the soup to a boil, then cover the pot and let it simmer for 30 minutes.

3. Blend the soup in a blender and return it to the pot. Add the milk and cheese. Reheat the soup, but do not allow it to boil again. Serve hot.

Harrira

(Moroccan Bean Soup)

Ingredients   *6–8 servings*

$^1/_2$ cup chickpeas, soaked overnight
$^1/_2$ cup lima beans
$^1/_2$ cup black beans, soaked overnight
$^1/_2$ cup red kidney beans, soaked overnight
$^1/_2$ cup lentils
$^1/_2$ cup split peas (yellow, if possible)
$^1/_2$ cup white navy beans, soaked overnight
12 cups water (more as needed)
2 large onions, chopped

1 16-ounce can tomatoes, chopped
$^1/_2$ teaspoon each, ginger, turmeric, cumin, cinnamon
$^1/_4$ teaspoon black pepper
1 tablespoon lemon juice
2 tablespoons flour
1 bunch fresh cilantro, chopped
8 leaves of fresh mint, chopped
salt to taste
pinch of cayenne
a good pinch of paprika

1. Place all the beans in a large pot, add the water, and bring it to a boil. Simmer for 1$^1/_2$ hours.

2. Add the onions, tomatoes with their juice, ginger, turmeric, cumin, cinnamon, black pepper, and lemon juice. Stir well, cover the pot, and bring the soup to a second boil. Reduce the heat to low-medium and simmer the soup for another hour.

3. Add the salt and more water if necessary. Dissolve the flour in a quarter cup of cold water and make a paste. Add a few tablespoons of the hot soup, mix thoroughly, and pour into the soup. Stir vigorously and continually so that the soup gradually thickens but without any lumps.

4. Add the cilantro (or parsley) and mint, cayenne powder, and paprika. Stir well and cook over low heat for 15 to 20 minutes. Serve hot.

This is the original fragrant soup from ancient Morocco. There, it is traditionally served during the 30-day Ramadan fast just before sunset, when the daily fast is broken once to strengthen the faster for the next day's fast.

Butternut Squash Soup Portuguese Style

Ingredients   *6 servings*

6 tablespoons olive oil
3 onions, chopped
5 garlic cloves, minced
2 butternut squash, peeled, halved, seeded, and cut in chunks
1 potato, peeled and cubed

1 carrot, peeled and sliced
7 cups vegetable or chicken stock
salt and pepper to taste
$1/3$ cup freshly minced parsley
fresh thyme leaves as garnish

1. Pour the olive oil into a large soup pot and sauté the onions and garlic over low heat for 3 to 5 minutes. Turn off the heat, cover the pot, and let the onion-garlic mixture steam for 15 minutes.

2. Add the squash, potato, and carrot and stir the mixture well. Pour the stock and bring the soup to a boil. Reduce the heat, cover the pot, and let it simmer for 45 minutes.

3. Add the seasonings and parsley stir well, cover the pot, and continue simmering for another 15 minutes.

4. Blend one third of the soup at a time in a blender or food processor and return it to the original but clean pot. Reheat the soup over low heat, but do not let it come to a boil. Serve hot and sprinkle fresh thyme leaves on top of each serving as garnish.

Soup Julienne

3 leeks (white part only)
3 carrots
3 medium-sized turnips
1/2 medium-sized head cabbage, shredded
1 onion

3 quarts water or vegetable or chicken stock
3 bouillon cubes of choice (if stock is not used)
salt and pepper to taste
1/3 cup minced parsley

1. Wash and rinse the vegetables. Slice them julienne style. Place them in a good-sized soup pot and add the water. Add the bouillon cubes and bring the water to a boil. Reduce the heat to medium, cover the pot, and cook the soup slowly for about 60 minutes, stirring from time to time.

2. When the soup is done, add salt, pepper, and parsley, and stir a few times, then cover the pot and simmer for 5 minutes more. Serve hot.

April

"'Sing a song of Spring,' cried the pleasant April rain
With a thousand sparkling tones upon the window pane,
And the flowers hidden in the ground woke dreamily and stirred,
From root to root, from seed to seed, crept swiftly the happy word."

—Celia Thaxter

Cream of Mushroom Soup à la Romaine

Ingredients   *4 servings*

4 tablespoons butter or margarine
1/2 pound chopped mushrooms
1 onion, chopped
1 carrot, sliced
2 garlic cloves, minced
pinch of thyme

2 tablespoons flour
1 quart water
salt and pepper to taste
1 pint cream
grated Romano cheese

1. Melt the butter in a soup pot. Add the mushrooms, onion, carrot, garlic, and thyme. Cover the pot and let the vegetables simmer for 5 minutes over very low heat.

2. Add the flour and stir well. Add the water, stir some more, and bring the soup to a quick boil. Over low heat, simmer for a half hour.

3. Blend the soup in the blender and then return it to the soup pot. Add the seasonings and cream and mix well. Reheat the soup, but do not let it boil again. Serve the soup hot and sprinkle grated Romano cheese on top of each bowl.

"Mushrooms of one night be the best
and they be little and red within
and closed at the top;
and they must be peeled
and then washed in hot water
and then parboiled
and if you wish to put them in a pasty
add oil, cheese, and spice powder."
— The Goodman of Paris (*Le Ménagier de Paris*)

Sweet Milk Soup for Children

Ingredients   *4 servings*

2 cups water
2 cups bread cubes
2 cups milk
¼ cup raisins

4 tablespoons real maple syrup
2 beaten eggs
dash nutmeg

1. Pour the water into the soup pot, add the bread, and bring to a boil, then simmer for 10 minutes.

2. Add the milk, raisins, and maple syrup. Stir well and bring the soup to a second boil. Add the beaten eggs and nutmeg. Blend well and simmer for 10 more minutes before serving.

This soup is a simple concoction that children have enjoyed throughout the ages. It has been prepared and served by mothers in a thousand different ways — e.g., using wild honey instead of syrup or berries instead of raisins. It has always lived up to young children's expectations and filled their hearts with utter delight.

Potage Villageois

(Village Vegetable-Macaroni Soup)

Ingredients   *6 Servings*

3 leeks
4 tablespoons butter or margarine
1 small cabbage
6 cups water
1 bouillon cube
6 potatoes, cubed

1 cup small macaroni noodles
2 cups milk
salt and pepper to taste
minced parsley
grated Parmesan cheese

1. Slice the leeks and cabbage julienne style and sauté them in butter for a few minutes over low heat.

2. Add the water and bouillon cube. Add the cubed potatoes. Bring the water to a boil and cook over medium heat for 30 minutes.

3. While the soup is boiling, cook the macaroni in a separate pot. When it is cooked, drain.

4. Add to the soup the cooked macaroni, milk, salt, pepper, and minced parsley. Allow the soup to come to a boil and then turn down the heat. Keep the cover on the pot and allow the soup to simmer for a few minutes. Serve the soup hot and garnish it at the last minute with grated Parmesan cheese.

This is a typical soup often served in the evening throughout the old villages of France — hence the name. It is a French version of the Italian minestrone, and other vegetables, like carrots or beans, may be added to it. Very often the French prefer the use of spaghetti-type noodles instead of macaroni for the preparation of this soup. If you decide to use spaghetti, break the noodles in half for easier eating.

Borscht

---

2 red beets

2 carrots

2 potatoes

2 leeks

½ head red cabbage

10 mushrooms

1 onion

2 tomatoes

3 ½ quarts water

4 tablespoons olive oil

salt and pepper

heavy cream or sour cream (1 tablespoon per serving)

finely minced parsley

1. Wash and peel the beets, carrots, and potatoes. Dice them into small cubes. Cut the leeks, cabbage, mushrooms, onion, and tomatoes into small pieces.

2. In a large soup pot, bring water to a boil, then add the oil and all the vegetables. Cover and cook over low-medium heat for about 30 minutes. Add salt and pepper to the soup and stir. Let the soup sit for 15 minutes, covered.

3. Reheat the soup for a few minutes and serve hot, adding 1 tablespoon of heavy cream and some minced parsley to the center of each serving.

Sour Cream Soup

Ingredients   *4–6 servings*

6 medium potatoes, peeled
6 cups water
3 large bay leaves
1 1/2 tablespoons caraway seeds (or
    to taste)
salt to taste

1/8 cup flour (or more if necessary)
1/2 cup milk
1 pint (16 ounces) sour cream (more
    if needed)
chopped scallions as garnish

1. Dice the potatoes very small and put them into the soup pot with the water. Add the bay leaves, caraway seeds, and salt. Cook until the potatoes are done. Do not drain the water.

2. Stir the flour into the milk and make a paste. Pour this mixture into the soup, stirring constantly while adding. This will thicken the soup.

3. Add the sour cream to the soup, stirring constantly while adding. Let the soup again come to a boil and then simmer it slowly for about 10 minutes. Remove the bay leaves and serve hot or cold. Add some chopped scallions as garnish on top of each serving.

"You must observe in all broths and soups that one thing does not taste more than another; but that the taste be equal, and it has a fine agreeable relish, according to what you design it for; and you must be sure that all greens and herbs you put in be cleaned, washed and picked."

—Hanna Glasse, *The Art of Cookery*, 1776

Potage Germiny

(Sorrel Soup)

Ingredients   *6 servings*

8 cups chicken or beef stock
4 tablespoons butter or margarine
5 cups thinly chopped and shredded
    sorrel leaves (about 20 leaves)

4 tablespoons finely chopped chervil
3 egg yolks
1 cup half-and-half
salt and pepper to taste

1. Place the stock in a large soup pot and cook over low-medium heat. Reduce heat gradually.

2. Melt the butter in a separate pot and add the chopped sorrel. Cook over low heat until the sorrel is tender and turns into a sauce. Add the chervil, blend well, and turn off the heat.

3. Place the egg yolks and half-and-half in a deep bowl and mix them well. Pour this mixture into the soup stock and mix it well. Do not let it reach the boiling point.

4. Add the sorrel-chervil mixture and also the seasonings to the soup. Stir and mix well. Serve hot or refrigerate and serve cold, depending on the season.

Cream of Curry Potage

Ingredients
6 servings

6 tablespoons crème fraîche
2 tablespoons curry powder
4 egg yolks
1 lemon

6 cups chicken stock (or vegetable)
salt to taste
croutons as garnish (see recipe
  p. 195)

1. In a large, deep bowl, place the crème fraîche, curry, egg yolks, and juice from the lemon. Mix thoroughly with a electric mixer.

2. Put the stock in a soup pot and bring it to a boil. Fill one cup with the stock and pour it over the egg-curry mixture. Mix well.

3. Pour the contents of the bowl into the boiling stock and continue to boil for 3 to 4 minutes, stirring constantly.

4. Place 4 croutons in each soup plate or bowl. Pour the soup over them and serve at once.

"Soup is a mainstay of civilization. It is a creative synthesis of flavors and textures, served in a comforting, back to childhood style; or as a precise and perfectly elegant beginning to the shape of things to come."

— Liz Smith

Shrimp Soup de Luxe

Ingredients

4 tablespoons olive oil
2 onions, minced
8 ounces tiny fresh or frozen shrimp
1 cup dry white wine
1 cup water
1/2 teaspoon dry mustard

3 cups milk (low fat can be used)
1 cup fresh chopped herbs: dill,
   chives, tarragon, and parsley
salt and white pepper to taste
sour cream as garnish

1. Heat the olive oil in a soup pot. Add the onions and shrimp. Cook and stir continually for about 5 minutes until both the shrimp and the onions look soft and tender.

2. Add the wine, water, and mustard and bring the soup to a boil. Lower the heat to medium and continue cooking for another 10 to 15 minutes.

3. Add the milk and seasonings and continue to cook the soup slowly for another 15 minutes. Stir often. Just before serving, add the cup of chopped herbs, mix well, and then ladle the soup into soup plates or bowls. Garnish with a teaspoon of sour cream on top of each serving.

A dear friend of mine who shared this recipe with me assures me that every time he serves this soup he gets wonderful compliments from his guests. The soup captures the rich, sweet taste of the shrimp, which are well complemented by the taste of the fresh herbs. This soup makes an ideal first course to an elegant dinner.

Three Peppers Soup

Ingredients 4 servings

3 peppers, 1 red, 1 yellow, and
   1 green
4 garlic cloves
5 teaspoons olive oil
5 cups beef or vegetable stock (or
   water and 3 bouillon cubes)

1/3 teaspoon saffron
8 slices bread (2 for each person)
4 eggs
salt and white pepper to taste
paprika as garnish

1. Broil the peppers. Let them cool and then peel them. Cut them in long, thin strips. Peel and chop garlic cloves.

2. Heat the oil in a soup pot and add the peppers and garlic. Cook for 1 minute, stirring continually. Add the stock and the saffron, stir some more, cover the pot, and cook over moderate heat for about 30 minutes.

3. Toast the bread slices and place them on a plate. Break the eggs and place them individually one by one into the soup. (Do this carefully so as to keep them whole). Add salt and pepper if desired.

4. Turn off the heat. Cover the pot and let the soup rest for 5 minutes, until the egg whites are cooked. Carefully place 2 slices of bread into each soup bowl, place 1 egg on top, and then cover them with the rest of the soup. Sprinkle some paprika on top and serve immediately.

"I regard cold hors d'oeuvres as quite unnecessary in a dinner; I even consider them counter to the dictates of common sense, and they are certainly injurious to the flavor of the soup that follows."
— August Escoffier

Cream of Asparagus Soup

Ingredients

2 quarts water
1/2 pound asparagus, tough ends
   removed, cut into 1-inch lengths
1 potato, peeled and diced
1 onion, sliced

1 medium carrot, sliced
1 cup heavy cream
2 tablespoons butter or margarine
salt and pepper to taste

1. Cook the vegetables in the boiling, salted water until they are tender. Pass the soup through a sieve or blend in a blender.

2. Return the soup to the pot, add the heavy cream, butter, salt, and pepper and stir, bringing the soup to a boil. Stir again. Cover the pot and let the soup simmer for another 10 minutes. Serve hot.

If one wishes the soup to be of a thicker consistency, one can easily substitute 1 cup of white sauce (see recipe p. 194) for the heavy cream.

Saint Joseph Chickpea Soup

Ingredients

2 cups chickpeas
10 cups water
2 cups canned tomatoes
1 large onion, chopped
1 stalk celery, minced
2 carrots, sliced

4 cloves of garlic, minced
1 red pepper, diced
4 tablespoons olive oil
1 bouillon cube
1 bay leaf
salt and pepper to taste

1. Soak chickpeas overnight. Boil them in plenty of water, add all the remaining ingredients, and cook slowly over medium heat for about 1 hour, until the peas and all the vegetables are tender.

2. Add salt and pepper. Simmer the soup, covered, for about 15 minutes. Remove the bay leaf before serving. Serve hot.

Saint Joseph, Jesus' foster father, is the patron of fathers of families, bursars and procurators, manual workers, especially carpenters, the Universal Church, and those who pray for a holy death. Always honored by followers of the monastic path, including Saint Teresa of Avila, he is the saint to whom monks and nuns make recourse whenever there is a serious financial problem in a monastery. His feast is celebrated on March 19, and he has an additional feast day on May 1, as Saint Joseph the Worker.

Cuban Black Bean Soup

Ingredients   *6–8 servings*

1 pound dried black beans
12 cups water
1/2 cup olive oil
3 onions, chopped
1 bell pepper, chopped
6 garlic cloves, minced
1 teaspoon thyme

1/2 teaspoon oregano
1 bay leaf
3 teaspoons sugar
4 teaspoons vinegar
salt and pepper to taste
pinch of cumin

1. Soak the beans overnight. Rinse the beans and discard the water. Place the beans and 12 cups of water in a large soup pot. Bring the water to a boil, lower the heat, cover the pot, and cook the beans slowly for 1 hour or until the beans are tender.

2. Pour the oil into a separate pot, add the onions, pepper, and garlic cloves, and sauté them lightly for about 2 to 3 minutes.

3. Take out 1 cup of cooked beans from the large pot and purée them in a blender. Add the purée to the sautéed vegetables and mix well. Add the whole mixture to the rest of the beans in the soup pot.

4. Add the thyme, oregano, bay leaf, sugar, vinegar, salt, pepper, and cumin. Stir well, cover the pot, and simmer for about 45 to 50 minutes. Remove the bay leaf and let the soup stand, covered, for another 10 minutes. Serve hot.

Vermicelli Soup

2 1/2 quarts water
4 vegetable bouillon cubes
3 garlic cloves, minced
1 onion, thinly sliced and minced
2 carrots, cut in small cubes

3 ounces vermicelli noodles
1/2 cup fresh parsley, minced
salt to taste
grated cheese of choice

1. Pour the water into a soup pot and bring it to a boil. Add the bouillon, garlic, and the cut-up vegetables and cook them for about 25 minutes. Add the vermicelli noodles and continue cooking for another 10 minutes over medium heat.

2. Add the minced parsley and salt. Cover the pot and simmer the soup for 5 more minutes before serving. Sprinkle grated cheese on the top of each soup plate or bowl just before serving. Serve hot.

Brussels Sprout Cream Potage

Ingredients   *6–8 servings*

2 tablespoons butter or margarine
1 pound Brussels sprouts, sliced into
  quarters
1 pound potatoes, peeled and diced
2 leeks or onions, sliced
3 garlic cloves, minced

8 cups water
pinch of thyme
salt and pepper to taste
1 bay leaf
2 cups milk

1. Melt the butter in a saucepan and sauté the Brussels sprouts, potatoes, onions, and minced garlic for 1 or 2 minutes. Stir continuously. Add the water and seasonings and cook slowly over low-medium heat for 40 to 45 minutes, or until soup is done. Remove the bay leaf.

2. Cook separately from the above some Brussels sprouts sliced into 4 even quarters, to be used as garnish on top of the soup.

3. When the soup is done, add the milk and stir well. Blend the soup in a blender and serve hot. Garnish each serving with the Brussels sprouts.

May

"Upon the first of May,
With garlands fresh and gay,
With mirth and music sweet,
For such a season meet,
They passe their time away."

—16th-century Old English song

Russian Chtchavel

Ingredients

4–6 servings

12 ounces sorrel (20 leaves)
2 quarts water
2 garlic cloves
3 hard-boiled eggs
the juice of 1 lemon

1/2 pint heavy cream
salt to taste
1 cucumber, thinly sliced (fresh or pickled)
black bread cut into cubes

1. Chop the sorrel and put it in a soup pot. Add the water and bring to a boil. Lower the heat to low-medium and cook for 20 minutes.

2. While the sorrel is cooking, chop the garlic and hard-boiled eggs. Add the garlic, eggs, and juice of the lemon to the soup. Continue cooking for 15 minutes.

3. Just before serving, add the heavy cream, salt, and cucumber. Stir well.

4. Place the bread cubes in the soup bowls and pour the soup over the bread. Serve hot.

Russian cookery is known for its abundance of soups. The long and severe winters make it imperative for the Russian people to think of heartwarming soups using every kind of produce available. Throughout the centuries, they have used their imagination and industriousness to test and discover suitable ways to use fresh, pickled, spicy, cured, or dry vegetables, as well as fruits, berries, mushrooms, meat, bread, and dairy products in their soups. Chtchavel is an example of the resourcefulness of the Russians in soup making.

Potage Clamart

(Turnip-Leek Potage)

Ingredients   *4 servings*

6 tablespoons oil of choice or butter
  or margarine
1 cup fresh peas
1 carrot
1 turnip
2 leeks

1 quart water
salt to taste
thyme and rosemary to taste
1 egg yolk
2 teaspoons heavy cream

1. Wash and rinse vegetables. Cut carrot, turnip, and leeks in thin slices.

2. Pour the oil into the soup pot and add the peas, carrot, turnip, and leeks. Cook slowly over very low heat for 2 minutes. Stir continually.

3. Add 1 quart of water, pinch of salt, thyme, and rosemary. Cook the soup slowly, keeping it covered for 30 minutes. Turn off the heat and let the soup stand for 15 minutes.

4. Blend the soup in a blender or put it through a sieve and return it to the pot. Add the beaten egg yolk and heavy cream and stir well. Serve hot.

This potage originated in Clamart, which is one of the neighboring suburbs just outside the city of Paris. It is a very tasty potage, due in great part to the special flavor given by the fresh peas. Ideally, this soup should be prepared in early spring when the fresh peas are in season, or later in the fall, when fresh peas are again harvested. The beaten egg and the cream enhance the creamy nature of the soup. If the potage is being prepared for an elegant dinner party, it should be garnished with some finely chopped chervil or hard-boiled eggs, as a finishing touch.

Shaker-Style Soup

Ingredients

2 tablespoons butter or margarine

2 tablespoons flour

2 6-ounce cans tomato paste

1 onion, chopped and minced

4 teaspoons dill

salt and pepper to taste

2 ¹/₂ cups water

2 ¹/₂ cups milk

¹/₂ cup sour cream

1. Melt the butter or margarine in a soup pot. Add the flour. Stir and mix well. Add the tomato paste, chopped onion, dill, salt, pepper, and water. Stir constantly and bring to a boil, then simmer for 20 minutes.

2. Heat the milk separately, add the sour cream to the hot milk, and mix well. Pour the milk–sour cream mixture into the soup and blend well. Use fresh chopped dill as garnish on top of each serving and serve hot.

"Shaker cookery, like everything Shaker designed or Shaker created, is traditionally simple and functional. If it is gourmet gastronomy you seek, or some rare epicurean dainty, forget it. You won't find exotics among these recipes. What you will find are simple directions for the preparation of tested comestibles, each conceived with loving care, to be of delicious taste and a wholesome, satisfying nature. When you get right down to it, isn't that what good food is all about? The Shakers, bless them, have known it for over a hundred years."

—Martin Dibner

Asparagus-Orange Velouté

Ingredients   *4 servings*

1 pound asparagus, peeled and well washed

4 cups water

4 tablespoons butter or margarine

3 tablespoons flour

salt and white pepper

2 egg yolks

1 cup dry white wine

2 tablespoons crème fraîche (or sour cream)

1 teaspoon sugar

1/2 cup freshly squeezed orange juice

pinch nutmeg

1. Peel the hard part of the asparagus and wash it well. Place the asparagus in a soup pot, add water, and cook at a gentle boil for 20 minutes. Drain the asparagus and preserve the water. Cut the asparagus stalks in half and place the top portions aside.

2. Melt the butter or margarine in another pot, add the flour a little at a time, and stir continuously. Add the water from the asparagus, the asparagus bottoms, salt, and pepper, and cook for 5 or 6 minutes, stirring continuously.

3. Blend the soup in a blender and return it to the soup pot. Continue cooking it over very low heat, not allowing the soup to come to a boiling point.

4. Beat the egg yolks in a deep bowl, add the wine, crème fraîche, and sugar and mix thoroughly. Pour this mixture into the soup. Add the orange juice, nutmeg, and asparagus tops and check the seasonings. Stir well and reheat the soup for a few minutes until it is hot. Don't let it boil. Serve immediately.

This is a light, tasty, and elegant velouté, to be served during an intimate dinner party. It is particularly attractive in early spring, when asparagus is in season. The orange juice blends wonderfully with the taste of the fresh asparagus.

Cabbage Soup

Ingredients   *6–8 servings*

3 quarts water   1 bouillon cube
1 head cabbage   1 teaspoon each parsley, thyme, and
3 leeks or onions   marjoram to taste
2 celery stalks   salt and pepper to taste
2 medium potatoes

1. Place the water in a large soup pot. Shred the cabbage and slice the leeks and celery. Add them to the water.

2. Peel and dice the potatoes. Add the potatoes and bouillon cube to the soup. Cover the pot and allow the soup to cook slowly over low-medium heat for at least 2 hours. Add more water if necessary.

3. When the soup is done, add the parsley, thyme, marjoram, salt, and pepper. Cover the pot and let the soup stand for 30 minutes before serving.

Cabbage is one of the most utilized vegetables in both northern Europe and America. In France it is also popular, especially in the northeastern corner of the country, near the German and Belgian borders. This classic soup probably originated in that area. It is hearty and filling and can be used as a complete meal. It is particularly appetizing on a cold winter night.

Potage Céline

(Carrot-Celeriac Soup)

Ingredients *6–8 servings*

4 ounces butter or margarine (or oil
   of choice)
1 pound carrots
$^1/_2$ pound celeriac

1 onion
2 quarts water
salt and pepper to taste
chervil (or parsley), well chopped

1. Melt the butter in a soup pot. Add carrots, celeriac, and onion sliced very thin or cut julienne style. Sauté vegetables for a few minutes and then add water.

2. Cook for a half hour, then add the salt and pepper according to taste. Stir well.

3. Blend the soup in a blender, then put it back into the pot and continue to cook slowly over low heat for about 15 to 20 minutes. Simmer a few minutes more.

4. Just before serving, add the chopped chervil and mix well. Serve hot, or chill for about 2 hours and serve cold. If soup is to be served cold, use oil instead of butter.

Cream of Broccoli Soup

Ingredients

1 pound fresh broccoli	1 cup heavy cream or half-and-half
3 medium-sized potatoes	salt to taste
2 onions	pinch of cayenne
8 cups water	grated cheese of choice as garnish
1 bouillon cube	

1. Wash, peel, and slice the vegetables into small pieces. Pour the water into a large soup pot and add all the vegetables and the bouillon. Cook slowly over medium heat for 1 hour.

2. Blend the soup in a blender and return it to the pot. Add the cream, salt, and cayenne and stir. Reheat for a few minutes and serve hot with grated cheese as garnish.

During the warm weather, this soup can be refrigerated for a few hours and then served cold. When the soup is served hot, you can sprinkle some grated cheese on top of each serving.

Broccoli is unfortunately not a preferred vegetable among many people, in spite of its rich nutritional value. Not only is broccoli full of vitamins and minerals, but recent studies suggest eating it may prevent certain cancers, such as breast and colon cancer. Many people find broccoli more acceptable to the palate when served in the form of a creamy soup such as this one. Try it to teach your loved ones to love broccoli.

Irish Brotchan Soup

4 tablespoons butter or margarine
4 leeks, chopped
4 parsnips, chopped
4 big potatoes, diced
7 cups water or stock (chicken or vegetable; add more if necessary)
2 bouillon cubes (not necessary if stock is used)

$^1/_2$ cup chopped parsley
3 tablespoons lemon juice
3 tablespoons white wine
salt and pepper to taste
6 teaspoons sour cream as garnish
scallions, finely chopped, as garnish

1. Melt the butter in a soup pot and sauté the leeks slowly for a few minutes. Stir frequently. Add the parsnips and potatoes. Stir some more, cover the pot, and continue the sautéing for another 2 minutes.

2. Add the water or stock, the bouillon cubes, parsley, lemon juice, wine, salt, and pepper. Bring the soup to a boil, place the lid over the pot, and simmer slowly for 40 minutes.

3. Let the soup cool, and then pass it through a sieve or blend in a blender. Return the soup to the pot. Check the seasonings, adding more lemon juice, salt, or pepper if necessary. Reheat the soup until it becomes very hot. Turn off the heat, cover the pot, and let the soup rest for 5 minutes before serving. Put 1 teaspoon of sour cream at the center of each serving and surround it with finely chopped scallions as garnish. Serve immediately.

Minestrone Monastico

3 quarts water

3 carrots

3 potatoes

1 cup green beans

2 celery stalks

1 cup dry white beans

3 onions

1 cup olive oil

1 cup dry white wine

1 cup macaroni

tarragon, minced

salt and pepper to taste

grated Parmesan cheese

1. Wash and peel the vegetables and cut them into small pieces (except the dry beans). Pour the water into a large soup pot and add all the vegetables (including beans) except the onions. Cook slowly over medium heat for 1 hour.

2. Sauté the onions in a bit of the olive oil in a large frying pan. When the onions begin to become golden, turn off the heat.

3. To the soup, add the onions, wine, the rest of the olive oil, macaroni, tarragon, salt, and pepper and continue cooking for another 15 minutes. Cover the pot and allow the soup to simmer for 10 minutes. Serve hot, with a side dish of grated Parmesan cheese.

In Italy, there are probably a thousand ways to prepare minestrone soup. Every household has a formula of its own. Minestrone has become quite popular in America and is often served at the monastic table as well. This particular version is proper to our monastery — hence the title of the recipe. Among the ingredients listed is a single cup of white wine, but one can easily add a cup or two more. The wine is the secret ingredient of this recipe — it makes all the difference in the world.

Potage Printanier à la Française

(French Spring Vegetable Soup)

Ingredients   *6–8 servings*

3 tablespoons butter or margarine
2 cups chopped cauliflower
1 cup fresh peas
1 cup chopped spinach
2 sliced carrots
2 leeks
1 chopped celeriac
2 quarts water, or more, if necessary

1 cup sherry wine or white wine of
   choice
2 bouillon cubes
2 sliced tomatoes, peeled and
   chopped
pinch mixed herbs (parsley, chervil,
   and thyme)
salt and pepper to taste

1. Melt the butter in a soup pot and sauté the above vegetables for 1 or 2 minutes, except the tomatoes.

2. Add the water, sherry, bouillon cubes, peeled and chopped tomatoes, mixed herbs, salt, and pepper. Cook the soup slowly, covered, over low-medium heat for about 1 hour. Stir from time to time and add more water if necessary. Let the soup sit for 10 minutes.

3. When ready to serve, add some more fresh finely chopped herbs. Serve hot.

"Soup and fish explain half of the emotions of life."
— Sydney Smith

Saint Germain Pea Soup

Ingredients

1 pound yellow or green split peas   1 large onion, sliced
8 cups water   1 bay leaf
2 potatoes, peeled and diced   2 bouillon cubes
2 medium-sized turnips, diced   6 tablespoons olive oil or butter
2 medium carrots, diced   salt and pepper to taste
2 celery stalks, thinly sliced   croutons (see recipe p. 195)

1. Soak the peas as directed on package and then drain. Put the water for the soup into a large soup pot and bring it to a boil. Add the peas to the water. Also add the vegetables, bay leaf, and bouillon cubes. Cook over medium heat, covered, for about 1 hour, stirring from time to time. Let the soup cool.

2. Remove the bay leaf and blend the soup in a blender until it turns into a smooth cream. Pour the soup back into the pot. Add the oil, salt, pepper, and extra water or milk according to your preference. Bring the soup to a boil again, stirring continuously, for 5 minutes. Let the soup sit, covered, for 5 minutes. Place the croutons in the individual soup plates and pour the soup on top of them. Serve hot.

Avocado Velouté

6 tablespoons butter

6 onions, sliced and minced

3 garlic cloves, minced

2 quarts water or broth

2 tablespoons brandy

4 eggs, with the yolks separated from the whites

2 avocados, peeled

6 tablespoons half-and-half or heavy cream

salt and pepper to taste

fresh cilantro, chopped finely

1. Melt the butter in a soup pot. Add the onions and garlic. Sauté slightly while stirring continually. Add the water and the brandy, cover the pot, and cook over low-medium heat for 30 minutes.

2. Blend the soup in a blender and return the contents to the pot. Beat the egg whites stiffly and add them to the soup while continuously stirring.

3. Place the egg yolks and the avocados in the blender and mix them thoroughly. Add this mixture, plus the salt and pepper, to the soup and continue stirring for a few minutes, until all the elements in the soup are well mixed. Continue cooking for 10 more minutes.

4. Add the half-and-half or cream and stir some more. Serve the velouté hot and sprinkle finely chopped cilantro on top as garnish.

Saint Christopher Soup

Ingredients   *6 servings*

8 cups vegetable broth (see recipe
 p. 192)
½ medium-sized red cabbage, finely
 shredded and minced

8 tablespoons lemon juice
salt and pepper to taste

1. Prepare a good vegetable broth.

2. Place the finely chopped cabbage, lemon juice, salt, and pepper in a deep bowl. Let the mixture sit for an hour, stirring from time to time.

3. Bring the broth to a boil, add the cabbage and all the contents of the bowl, and cook for about 5 minutes. Serve immediately after.

This is a wonderful curative soup that is often used in France to ease indigestion problems or hangovers. It is a common remedy for many illnesses.

June

"What is one to say about June....
the time of perfect young summer,
the fulfillment of the promise of the earlier months,
and with as yet no sign to remind one that its fresh
young beauty will never fade?
For my own part I wander up into the wood and say:
'June is here—June is here: thank God for lovely June!'"

— Gertrude Jekyll

Soup from the Ardennes

Ingredients   *4–6 servings*

3 medium potatoes
2 leeks (white parts only)
2 shallots
3 Belgian endives
3 ounces butter or margarine

6 cups milk (more if needed; can use
   skim)
salt and white pepper
nutmeg to taste
croutons (see recipe p. 195)

1. Peel the potatoes and cut them into thin slices. Slice the leeks, shallots, and endives very fine, julienne fashion.

2. Melt the butter in a saucepan, add the leeks, shallots, and endives, and sauté them for a few minutes. Add the milk and bring to a light boil. Add the potatoes, salt, pepper, and nutmeg. Lower the heat to low-medium and cook the soup for about 25 minutes, stirring from time to time.

3. Turn off the heat, cover the saucepan with a lid, and allow the soup to sit for 10 minutes.

4. Prepare croutons according to recipe on p. 195 or grill a few pieces of bread cubes to use as croutons. Place a few in each plate and pour the soup on top. Serve hot.

This is another soup that comes to us from the Belgian–northern French border. It is a soup that utilizes the classic vegetables of that region: leeks, endives, and potatoes. The very fact that the soup is prepared with milk rather than water enhances the quality and flavor of the soup. Those who may be concerned about the extra calories of the milk can easily substitute skim milk.

Cream of Fresh Greens Soup

Ingredients   *6 servings*

6 tablespoons olive oil
1 onion, chopped
1 head lettuce or escarole, finely
   chopped
1 bunch watercress, finely chopped
1 pound spinach, chopped
6 quarts water, more if necessary

2 bouillon cubes
2 potatoes, sliced
1 pint heavy cream
salt, nutmeg, and white pepper to
   taste
paprika as garnish

1. Pour the olive oil into the soup pot and sauté the onion slightly. Add the chopped greens, potatoes, bouillon cubes, and water. Boil the soup for 15 minutes and then simmer for another 15 minutes.

2. Blend the soup in a blender and return it to the pot. Add the heavy cream and seasonings and stir well. Reheat the soup and serve hot, sprinkling some paprika on top of each serving.

"Beautiful soup, so rich and green.
Waiting in a hot tureen!
Who for such dainties would not stoop?
Soup of the evening, beautiful soup!"
                —Lewis Carroll, *Alice in Wonderland*

Oyster and Mushroom Soup

Ingredients

1/2 cup shucked oysters
1/3 cup olive oil
2 shallots, chopped
1 1/2 cups mushrooms, thinly sliced
1 cup dry vermouth or white wine
3 cups milk

1/2 cup heavy cream
salt and pepper to taste
1 tablespoon tarragon
pinch dry mustard
grated lemon rind as garnish

1. Drain the oysters and place them aside.

2. Pour the oil into a pot and sauté the shallots and the mushrooms lightly for 2 to 3 minutes. Add the vermouth, stir well, cover pot, and continue cooking for 2 more minutes.

3. Add the oysters, milk, cream, salt, and pepper. Lower the heat to low-medium, cover the pot, and simmer the soup slowly for 20 minutes. Stir frequently and be sure the soup is boiling only very lightly.

4. Add the tarragon and a pinch of dry mustard. Stir well, cover the soup, and let it rest for 5 minutes before serving. Serve hot. Grate a lemon rind on top of the soup as garnish.

Danish Onion–Champagne Soup

Ingredients   *6–8 servings*

10 onions, sliced

5 tablespoons butter or margarine or
   oil of choice

4 cups boiling water

2 bay leaves

salt and fresh ground pepper to taste

dash cayenne pepper and nutmeg

1 quart dry champagne

half a Camembert cheese (or small
   Brie)

4 yolks of eggs

1 cup port wine

8 slices bread fried in butter

1. Sauté the onions in butter until they begin to turn golden. Add the cups of boiling water, salt, pepper, and a dash of cayenne and nutmeg. Add also the bay leaves. Stir well and bring the water to another boil. Reduce the heat to low-medium and cook, covered, for 20 minutes.

2. Add the entire bottle of champagne and bring the soup to yet another boil. Then add the cheese and take care to mix it well in the boiling soup.

3. Beat the egg yolks together with the port wine and add the egg-wine mixture to the soup. Stir well. Turn off the heat and let the soup rest, covered, for 10 minutes. (The soup must not boil again after the egg-wine mixture has been added).

4. Place 1 slice of fried bread in the center of each bowl and ladle the soup on top of it. Serve hot.

Northern Europe is well known for soups made with beer. This soup from Denmark, however, makes use of champagne, which gives the soup a particular flavor all its own. Since champagne is expensive, I recommend a local, more ordinary type of sparkling wine, not the costly authentic champagne imported from France. This is an excellent soup to serve when one has a congenial and informal group of friends over for a meal. But since it is quite heavy, the rest of the menu should be light though equally appetizing.

Potato Dumpling Soup

Ingredients

Ingredients   *4 servings*

1 onion
1 carrot
1 celery stalk
4 mushrooms
6 tablespoons oil
5 cups water
salt and pepper to taste

Dumplings:
1 1/2 cups mashed potatoes
1 teaspoon salt
1 egg
1 tablespoon chopped parsley
1/2 cup flour

1. Slice the vegetables thinly and sauté them slowly in the oil for a few minutes in a soup pot. Add the water gradually, stirring continuously. Add salt and pepper. Cover the pot and cook over low-medium heat for 30 minutes.

2. While the soup is cooking, combine all the ingredients for the dumplings. Roll the paste into a thin long cylinder. Cut into 1-inch lengths and roll them in the palms of your hands.

3. Drop the dumplings into the soup and continue cooking for another 8 to 10 minutes. Serve hot.

Greek Spartan Soup

4 cups beef broth

8 cups water

2 leeks, sliced julienne style

2 carrots, sliced julienne style

1 celery stalk, thinly sliced

1 small cabbage, shredded

1 large onion, sliced

1 garlic clove, minced

2 lemons

4 eggs

salt and pepper to taste

1. Pour the broth and the water into a large soup pot. Add all the vegetables and bring to a gentle boil. Lower the heat to low-medium and simmer the soup for 1 1/2 hours, covered. Add more water, if needed. Skim all the white part that rises in the soup carefully and discard it.

2. Squeeze the juice from the 2 lemons and add it to the soup. Beat the eggs carefully and mix them with the soup. Add the seasonings and stir quickly for 2 or 3 minutes. Serve the soup immediately.

Despite its name, there is nothing "Spartan" about this soup. Everyone who has tried this recipe assures me it is very rich and very filling. This soup is a complete meal in itself, or a repas complet, as it is called in France. The eggs add a full meal's worth of protein. A light salad of mixed greens and a piece of fresh fruit following the soup should be enough to satisfy anyone, no matter how hungry.

Chervil Soup

2 leeks
1/2 cup chopped celery
2 tablespoons butter, margarine, or
   oil of choice
4 potatoes, diced

1 quart water
2 cups milk
1 1/2 cups fresh chopped chervil
salt and pepper to taste

1. Wash and cut the leeks and celery into thin pieces. Melt the butter in a soup pot. Add the leeks, celery, and potatoes. Sauté for 2 to 3 minutes. Add the water and cook, covered, over low-medium heat until the soup is done.

2. Add the remaining ingredients and purée the soup in a blender. Bring the soup to a boil again, stirring continuously. Serve immediately. Soup can also be refrigerated and served cold during the hot weather.

Solyanka

(Cucumber-Fish Soup)

2 large cucumbers (fresh or pickled)
3 tablespoons butter or margarine
2 onions, chopped
6 cups water
$1/2$ cup vodka
2 white fish fillets (cod or haddock),
    cut into small chunks
1 bay leaf

2 teaspoons chopped capers
$1/4$ cup green olives, pitted and
    chopped
salt and pepper to taste
garnish: 1 lemon cut in thin slices,
    fresh parsley (or dill), finely
    chopped

1. Peel and halve the cucumber. Scoop out the seeds. Cut the cucumber into thin slices, sprinkle them with salt, and place them in a bowl in the refrigerator for at least 8 hours. Rinse and drain the slices before adding them to the soup.

2. Melt the butter in a soup pot and sauté the onions over moderate heat for 2 to 3 minutes. Add the water, vodka, fish chunks, and bay leaf. Bring the water to a boil, cover the pot, and cook the soup for 20 minutes.

3. Add the cucumber slices, capers, olives, salt, and pepper. Cover the pot and simmer for another 20 minutes.

4. Turn off the heat, remove the bay leaf, and serve the soup immediately. Garnish each plate with 2 lemon slices and some finely chopped parsley.

"The classification of traditional Russian soups has been traced to 16th and 17th century annals. Solyanka was originally applied to any food by the peasantry. Today Solyanka denotes a savoury, tart soup in which sauerkraut or pickled cucumbers are one of the main ingredients."

—F. Siegel, *Russian Cooking*

Cream of Cauliflower Soup

1 pound fresh cauliflower
2 potatoes
1 large carrot
1 onion
2 garlic cloves, chopped

1 bouillon cube
8 cups water
2 cups white sauce (see recipe p. 195)
salt and pepper to taste
chopped chervil as garnish

1. Wash vegetables and slice into small pieces. Put the water in a large pot and add all the vegetables, the chopped garlic, and the bouillon cube. Cook slowly, covered, over low-medium heat for 1 hour. Add more water if necessary.

2. In a medium-sized pot, prepare 2 cups of white sauce according to the recipe on p. 194.

3. After the vegetables are cooked, blend the soup in a blender and then pour back into the pot. Add the white sauce and seasonings according to taste. Stir the soup thoroughly.

4. Reheat the soup for a few minutes to serve hot (during the winter months). During the warm months, refrigerate the soup for 4 or more hours and serve cold. Sprinkle chopped chervil on top as garnish.

Cauliflower has a wonderful mild taste that doesn't overpower the palate. This particular soup can be prepared and enjoyed all year round, since fresh cauliflower is readily available everywhere. If you decide to serve it during the summer months, then be sure to chill it first for several hours before serving.

Zuppa di Pasta e Fagioli

(Pasta and Bean Soup)

Ingredients   *4–6 servings*

2 medium-sized onions, finely chopped

1/3 cup olive oil

4 garlic cloves, minced

1 28-ounce can Italian tomatoes, chopped, with juice

1 bay leaf

1 teaspoon dried rosemary

1 teaspoon fresh or dried basil, chopped

4 sprigs fresh Italian parsley, chopped

4 cups precooked white beans (cannellini) or the equivalent in canned beans (1 15-ounce can cannellini beans)

6 cups water

1 cup white wine

salt and freshly ground pepper to taste

4 ounces dried pasta (small shells are best)

grated Parmesan or Romano cheese as garnish

1. Sauté the onions in olive oil in a large-sized soup pot for about 2 minutes. Add the garlic and sauté for another minute, stirring continually.

2. Add the chopped tomatoes (with their juice), bay leaf, rosemary, basil, and parsley. Cook over medium heat for about 3 minutes, until the mixture attains a smooth, thick consistency. Stir often.

3. Add the precooked beans, water, wine, salt, and pepper. Stir the soup well and bring it to a boil. Cook for about 15 minutes, covered, over medium heat. (Do not overcook.) Add the pasta and continue cooking for another 5 minutes. Turn off the heat, cover the pot, and let the soup rest for about 10 minutes. Serve hot. Remove the bay leaf. Sprinkle some grated cheese on the top of each serving. For that extra Italian touch, add 1 tablespoon olive oil in the center of the bowl.

Additions may be made to this soup, e.g., other vegetables or pancetta *(bacon), according to taste.*

Carrot Soup à la Normande

Ingredients *6 servings*

2 onions
8 carrots
6 cups water
1 cup milk
3 tablespoons flour

pinch of thyme
6 tablespoons olive oil
salt and pepper to taste
6 tablespoons lemon juice
finely minced parsley

1. Chop onions and carrots finely, put in soup pot, and add water. Cook slowly, bringing the water to a boil. Then let the soup sit, covered, for 20 minutes.

2. Add the milk, flour, thyme, oil, salt, and pepper. Blend in a blender and pour the soup back into the pot. Add the lemon juice. Cook slowly for about 10 minutes, until hot. Serve the soup with parsley sprinkled on top. It can be served hot or cold. (Refrigerate for a few hours if you decide to serve it cold.)

Exotic Chinese Cucumber Soup

Ingredients

6 cups chicken or vegetable broth

2 good-sized cucumbers, peeled, seeded, and diced

8 mushrooms, washed and thinly sliced

4 scallions, chopped

salt and pepper to taste

8 teaspoons sesame oil

1 tablespoon white vinegar or rice vinegar

pinch ginger powder

1. Place the broth in a soup pot and bring it to the boiling point. Add the cucumbers, mushrooms, scallions, salt, and pepper. Cover the soup pot and cook gently over low-medium heat for 15 to 20 minutes.

2. Blend the soup in a blender. Add the extra seasonings — sesame oil, vinegar, and ginger — and blend well. Refrigerate the soup for a few hours and serve cold. Or reheat the soup and serve it hot, as the Chinese do.

"For people not familiar with Chinese or Japanese broths, these can be described either as extremely delicate or as appearing to be made with no ingredients at all. Beef or chicken broth made according to Oriental recipes is like English beef tea made with lean soup meat and herbs and simmered for hours below the boiling point — this to keep the broth clear without having to strain it or clarify it with eggshells."

—Dolores Vanetti, *The Querulous Cook*

Spanish Cilantro Soup

6 tablespoons olive oil
2 onions, chopped
2 leeks (whites only), chopped
3 garlic cloves, minced
4 potatoes, peeled and cubed
7 cups vegetable or chicken broth

1 cup coarsely chopped fresh cilantro
   (or a very large bunch) — save
   some for garnish
salt to taste
pinch of cayenne pepper to taste

1. Pour the olive oil into a soup pot and sauté the onions, leeks, and garlic lightly over low heat for 2 to 3 minutes. Add the cubed potatoes and continue sautéing for 1 extra minute while stirring constantly.

2. Add the broth, cover the pot, and simmer the soup for 30 minutes, or until the potatoes are thoroughly cooked. Remove from the heat.

3. Add the fresh cilantro and also the salt and cayenne pepper. Blend the soup in a blender or food processor about one third of the amount at a time. Refrigerate the soup for at least 10 hours before serving. Serve the soup very cold with some fresh cilantro leaves on top of each serving as garnish.

Celery-Orange Velouté

---

8 celery stalks, chopped
6 cups water
4 cups orange juice
1 bouillon cube (vegetable)
salt and pepper to taste
2 egg yolks

$^1/_2$ cup white vermouth (dry)
1 teaspoon flour
2 tablespoons crème fraîche or sour
  cream
$^1/_2$ teaspoon sugar
fresh mint leaves as garnish

---

1. Wash, clean, and chop the celery stalks. Place them in a soup pot. Add the water, orange juice, bouillon cube, salt, and pepper. Bring to a boil, then cover the pot and cook at a gentle boil for 1 $^1/_2$ to 2 hours. Pass the soup through a colander and remove the solids.

2. Beat the egg yolks in a deep bowl. Add the vermouth, flour, crème fraîche, and sugar and mix thoroughly (better yet, blend it in a blender until thick and creamy).

3. Pour the mixture into the soup and stir thoroughly until it is all well blended. Check the seasonings and reheat the soup until it is hot. (Do not let it come to a boil!) Serve immediately, placing a few fresh mint leaves on each serving as garnish. (This soup is always refreshing, even when it is served hot during the summer months).

Chilled Carrot Soup

2 leeks, chopped
2 potatoes, peeled and diced
4 good-sized carrots, sliced
3 1/2 cups chicken or vegetable stock
salt to taste

1/2 teaspoon ginger powder
4 tablespoons lemon juice
1 cup half-and-half
thin slices of lemon or fresh mint
  leaves as garnish

1. Place the prepared vegetables in a soup pot, add stock and salt, and bring the soup to a boil. Reduce the heat and simmer, covered, until the vegetables are well cooked.

2. Add the ginger, lemon juice, and half-and-half. Stir well.

3. Blend the soup in a blender or food processor and then chill the soup for a few hours before serving. Serve the soup in glass bowls and garnish each with a thin lemon slice or with fresh mint leaves.

July

"O summer day beside the joyous sea!
O summer day so wonderful and white,
So full of gladness and so full of pain!
Forever and forever shalt thou be
To some the gravestone of a dead delight,
To some the landmark of a new domain."

— Henry Wadsworth Longfellow

Saint Bertille Herb Soup

Ingredients   *6 servings*

1 small head leaf lettuce
1 bunch sorrel
1 cup chopped parsley
10 scallions or 2 leeks
1 bunch watercress
butter
1 1/2 quarts water (or vegetable stock
   if served hot)

1 cup white wine
1/2 cup heavy cream or half-and-half
1 egg yolk, beaten
1/2 cup chervil
salt and pepper to taste

1. Shred the lettuce and the sorrel. Chop the parsley, scallions, and watercress into small pieces.

2. Melt the butter in the soup pot, add the chopped greens, and cook slowly for a few minutes over low heat. Stir continually. Add the water (or stock) and the wine. Cover the pot and cook for about 40 minutes.

3. Remove the pot from the heat, add the cream, beaten egg, chervil, salt, and pepper. Blend well in a blender. Reheat the soup for a few minutes, but do not allow it to boil. Refrigerate the soup and serve cold. Or it can be served hot with slices of French bread on the side.

"Many soups that evolved through the centuries, in the French provinces, are based more on vegetables than on meats and are described as 'healthy' potages de santé.... These soups depend on spinach and sorrel, and all the herbs, and mushrooms, and fresh milk and cream and butter, all tasting perennially and incredibly delicious after the long dark months of eating stored roots, like turnips, and potatoes and cabbages and onions and garlic."
—M. E. K. Fisher, *The Cooking of Provincial France*

Cream of Vegetable Soup
à la Mode de Tours

Ingredients   *6 servings*

4 large carrots
4 medium-sized white turnips
3 leeks (white parts only)
4 tablespoons butter, or margarine,
   or oil of choice
7 cups water
2 large potatoes, peeled and sliced

$^1/_2$ cup rice
$^1/_2$ cup peas, fresh or frozen
2 cups milk
salt and pepper to taste
crème fraîche and chopped chervil as
   garnish

1. Wash and slice finely the carrots, turnips, and leeks.

2. Melt the butter in a soup pot and sauté the vegetables briefly for 2 or 3 minutes. Stir continually. Add the water and bring it to a boil. Lower the heat to medium and cook, covered, for about 15 minutes.

3. Add the potatoes, rice, and peas and stir. Cover the pot and continue cooking for another 30 minutes, this time over low-medium heat.

4. Strain the soup and pass the vegetables through a sieve or blend in a blender. Return the liquid part and the vegetables to the soup pot. Add the milk and the seasonings and bring the soup to a light boil while stirring often. Turn off the heat and let the soup stand, covered, for 5 minutes. Serve the soup hot during the winter months or refrigerate for a few hours and serve it cold during the summer. If the soup is served cold, it is better to use a light oil instead of butter. Garnish the soup with a teaspoon of crème fraîche (or sour cream) at the center and some finely chopped chervil all around.

Consommé of Celeriac

Ingredients   *4–6 servings*

2–3 celeriacs   1 celery heart
2 quarts water   parsley
3 bouillon cubes, or chicken stock   pinch of cayenne
3 tomatoes   salt to taste
2 lemons

1. Cut the celeriacs into big chunks and cook them slowly in the water over medium heat. Add the bouillon cubes and continue to cook.

2. Peel the tomatoes and strain them through a colander, discarding the seeds. Add this mixture and the juice from the lemons to the soup.

3. Slice the celery heart into thin small pieces. Chop the parsley, then mince the celery and parsley together and add them to the soup. Add the cayenne and salt.

4. After 1 hour and 15 minutes of cooking, taste and see if the soup is done. Then strain it through a thin colander, separating the solid vegetables. Place the consommé in the refrigerator for several hours. Serve cold.

"With a knowledge of blended flavors, the French have combined imagination and a flair for seasoning, so that their soups are worthy of imitation."
—Claire de Pratz, *French Home Cooking*

Jerusalem Artichoke Soup

Ingredients

8 cups water

10 Jerusalem artichokes, well-washed and sliced

5 large potatoes, peeled and sliced

1 leek, thinly sliced

2 onions, chopped

2 garlic cloves, minced

6 tablespoons oil of choice or butter or margarine

salt and pepper to taste

2 cups milk

fresh chopped parsley as garnish

1. Pour water into a soup pot and add the Jerusalem artichokes and potatoes. Cover the pot, bring the water to a boil, and then reduce the heat to low-medium. Simmer gently for 45 minutes.

2. Slice the leek and onions and mince the garlic. Place them in a separate pot, add the oil or butter, and sauté over low heat with the pan covered for about 2 or 3 minutes, maximum. Stir frequently, and see that the vegetables don't burn or stick to the pan.

3. Add the leek-garlic-onion mixture to the soup and continue cooking for an added 15 minutes. Turn off the heat and allow the soup to cool.

4. Blend the soup in a blender or food processor or pass it through a sieve. Return the soup to a clean pot and add the seasonings and the milk. Mix well and reheat the soup, bringing it to a boil. Turn off the heat, cover the pot, and let the soup rest for 5 minutes before serving. Garnish each serving with fresh chopped parsley on the top. (This soup can be refrigerated for a few hours and served cold during the summer months.)

Colbert Clear Soup

2 quarts water
4 bouillon cubes
2 carrots
2 leeks or onions
1 bunch sorrel leaves (or spinach leaves)

2 tablespoons lemon juice
1/2 cup white vermouth
salt and pepper to taste

1. Bring the water to a boil. Add the bouillon cubes, sliced carrots, leeks, sorrel, lemon juice, vermouth, and salt and pepper. Cook soup slowly for 1 hour and 15 minutes. Let it stand for 15 minutes, then strain it through a colander.

2. Refrigerate the consommé for several hours and serve it very cold.

"All of us know that the water in which vegetables have been cooked contains valuable mineral matter. It hurts us to throw it out, but we do not want to serve it with the vegetables. The soup pot waits for such things, and in proportion as it receives them is the soup rich and tasty. Its success does not depend upon accurate measurements and specific ingredients but upon blended flavors."

—Claire de Pratz, *French Home Cooking*

Cold Tomato Soup

Ingredients   *4–6 servings*

1/3 cup olive oil
4 leeks (white part only)
8 large tomatoes
4 minced garlic cloves
8 cups water
bouquet garni (a few sprigs of
    tarragon, thyme, and basil tied
    together and removed before
    serving the soup)

Salt and pepper to taste
dash of lemon juice
1 celery stalk, chopped and minced
    (optional)

1. Pour the oil into a large soup pot. Add the sliced leeks, garlic, and tomatoes, peeled and sliced into quarters. Sauté for a few minutes until the tomatoes dissolve into a sauce.

2. Add water and the remaining ingredients. Cover the pot and let the soup cook over medium heat for about 30 minutes. Strain the soup through a sieve and refrigerate it for at least 3 hours. Serve very chilled.

Shrimp and Corn Chowder

Ingredients *6 servings*

5 cups water
2 onions, chopped
2 celery stalks, chopped
1 small chopped green pepper
1 finely diced carrot
2 large potatoes, diced
1 bay leaf
2 tablespoons flour

2 cups milk
1 17-ounce can creamed corn
1 cup whole-kernel corn
1 pound shelled shrimp, cooked
salt and pepper to taste
finely chopped parsley and paprika
  (as garnish)

1. Pour the water into a large soup pot. Add the onions, celery, pepper, carrot, potatoes, and bay leaf. Bring to a boil and then simmer slowly, covered, for about 20 minutes.

2. Dilute the flour in milk and add to the soup.

3. Add the corn, cooked shrimp, and seasonings. Blend and stir the soup, cooking for a few minutes over low-medium heat. Remove the bay leaf. Serve the soup, garnishing each bowl with a sprinkle of chopped parsley and paprika.

"In 15 intervening years I had forgotten how delicious was this shrimp and corn chowder. I have since made it with both fresh and frozen corn — and can hardly tell which is which. I have also used frozen shrimps with excellent results.... The thin white sauce that gives the chowder its special creaminess is made separately and brought together with the other ingredients in the preparation."
—Bernard Clayton, Jr., *The Complete Book of Soups and Stews*

Consommé Madrilène

Ingredients *4–6 servings*

8 cups water
4 bouillon cubes
4 celery stalks, sliced and minced
2 medium onions, minced
2 tomatoes, peeled and sliced

1 green pepper, sliced
1 10-ounce can tomato sauce
dash of cayenne
salt and pepper to taste

1. Bring the water to a boil and add bouillon cubes, prepared vegetables, the can of tomato sauce, cayenne, salt, and pepper. Boil slowly over low-medium heat for 1 hour 15 minutes. Let stand for another 10 minutes.

2. Strain the consommé through a colander. Refrigerate for several hours. Serve cold.

Avocado Soup

Ingredients

2 avocados (ripe)

1 cup skim milk (or light cream for a thicker soup)

4 tablespoons scallions, minced

1 teaspoon lemon juice

3 cups chicken broth

$1/4$ cup dry sherry

salt and white pepper to taste

$1/4$ cup cilantro, minced

1. Cut the avocados in half. Pit, peel, and cut them into chunks. Blend the avocado chunks and the milk in a blender. Add the scallions and lemon juice and blend again until the mixture becomes smooth.

2. Bring the chicken broth to a boil. Turn off the heat and add the sherry, salt, pepper, and half of the cilantro. Let it simmer for a few minutes.

3. Pour the avocado mixture into the broth and mix thoroughly. Allow the soup to be refrigerated for at least 2 hours. Serve the soup cold, and garnish with the remaining cilantro before serving.

This is a wonderful and nutritious soup for the summertime, and serves as a delectable appetizer to a good summer meal. Vegetarians may wish to substitute vegetable broth for the chicken broth. Nutrition-wise, keep in mind that avocado contains complete protein.

Cold Salmon Chowder

Ingredients   *4 servings*

1 quart low-fat milk (more if
  necessary)

1 onion, sliced

1 celery stalk, sliced

1 small red pepper, diced

1 cup fresh salmon, lightly poached

$^1/_2$ cup light cream

4 teaspoons dry sherry

salt and white pepper to taste

cucumber slices as garnish

some chopped dill

1. Pour the milk into a soup pot and cook thinly sliced vegetables for about 10 minutes, stirring continually.

2. Remove all the bones and skin from the salmon, flake it, and add it to the soup. Add the cream, sherry, and seasonings. With an electric mixer, blend the soup thoroughly. Place it in the refrigerator and chill it for at least 8 to 10 hours.

3. As you ladle the chowder into the soup plates, garnish each one with a cucumber slice and some finely chopped dill.

This is an easy recipe to prepare and serve during the hot days of summer. The word "chowder" has its roots in the French word chaudière, *a 3-legged heavy iron pot used to prepare thick soups. It is very probable that the word migrated from French Canada to New England and later to Long Island, New York, where all varieties of thick seafood soups go by the name of chowder.*

Pea and Carrot Minted Soup

5 cups peas, fresh or frozen

2 carrots, peeled and sliced

2 leeks, or 1 onion, chopped

5 cups vegetable or chicken stock

1 tablespoon sugar

8 fresh mint leaves

3 tablespoons butter or margarine or oil of choice

2 tablespoons cornstarch

1 cup milk (low-fat can be used)

salt and pepper to taste

fresh mint leaves as garnish

1. Place prepared vegetables in the soup pot and add the stock. Bring the soup to a boil, add the sugar, mint leaves, salt, and pepper, and then cover the pot. Simmer the soup over low heat for 30 minutes.

2. Blend the soup in a blender or food processor until it is thoroughly puréed.

3. Melt the butter in a separate pot, add the cornstarch, and stir continually until it turns into a paste. Add the milk and continue stirring until it thickens.

4. Add the sauce to the pea soup and blend thoroughly. Reheat the soup and serve it hot with a few mint leaves on the top of each serving as garnish. (This soup can also be refrigerated for a few hours and served cold).

Neapolitan Zucchini Soup

Ingredients   *6 servings*

7 small zucchinis, sliced
3 tablespoons butter
6 cups water
salt and pepper to taste
3 eggs

4 tablespoons grated Parmesan
    cheese
bunch of parsley and basil, finely
    chopped
croutons (optional; see recipe p. 195)

1. Place the finely sliced zucchinis in a good-sized soup pot. Add the butter and cook slowly over low heat for about 5 minutes. Stir constantly.

2. Add the water, salt, and pepper, bring to a boil, and continue cooking until the zucchinis are tender (about 20 minutes). Cover the pot.

3. Beat the eggs in a large bowl, add the cheese, chopped parsley, and basil, and mix it all thoroughly. Add the mixture to the soup and stir. Allow it to cook for another 4 to 5 minutes, maximum.

4. Serve hot, adding some croutons on top as garnish.

Cold Basil Soup

Ingredients *6 servings*

2 medium-sized cucumbers, peeled,
   seeded and sliced
3 green bell peppers (sweet), sliced
4 medium-sized tomatoes, sliced
1 white sweet onion, sliced
2 garlic cloves, peeled

25 basil leaves, washed
5 cups cold water
1 16-ounce container of plain yogurt
salt and pepper to taste
fresh basil leaves as garnish

1. Place the prepared vegetables, garlic, and basil leaves in a blender and mix all of it thoroughly.

2. Pour the contents of the blender into a large soup pot or a large bowl. Add the water, salt, pepper, and yogurt and mix all of it well by hand. Refrigerate the soup for at least 3 hours before serving.

3. Serve the soup in deep bowls. Place some fresh basil leaves in the center as garnish.

August

"The quiet August noon has come;
A slumbrous silence fills the sky,
The fields are still, the woods are dumb,
In glassy sleep the water lies.

"Beneath the open sky abroad,
Among the plants and breathing things,
The sinless, peaceful works of God,
I'll share the calm the season brings."

—William Cullen Bryant

Cream of Fennel Soup

1 leek, thinly sliced
1/3 cup olive oil
4 garlic cloves, minced
5 fennel bulbs, thinly sliced
8 tomatoes, peeled, seeded, and chopped
6 cups water (or vegetable or chicken stock)

3 bouillon cubes (if stock not available)
1/2 cup top greens from the fennel, chopped finely in a food processor
1 cup heavy cream or low-fat yogurt
salt and pepper to taste

1. Sauté the leeks in the oil until tender. Add immediately the garlic and the fennel. Stir well and cook for a few minutes, until the fennel begins to soften.

2. Add the tomatoes. Stir well and cook over moderate heat until the tomatoes are dissolved and turn into a sauce. Add the water or stock. Bring to a boil and cook over medium heat for 15 minutes.

3. Blend the soup in a blender and then return it to the soup pot. Add the processed fennel greens, cream, salt, and pepper. Bring to a boil again for 1 minute. Turn off the heat, stir well, cover the pot, and let the soup rest for 10 minutes before serving. During the summer months, chill the soup in the refrigerator for 1 hour and serve cold.

This is an unusual and elegant soup, usually served cold during the summer months. The licorice taste of the fennel is simultaneously subtle, refreshing, and striking. Fat-watchers may easily substitute low-fat yogurt for the heavy cream. Or, better yet, use a half cup of regular yogurt and a half cup of low-fat milk.

Garlic Consommé

Ingredients   *6 servings*

2 quarts water (or meat stock)
3 bouillon cubes (if stock not used)
12 cloves garlic, minced
1 bouquet garni (bay leaf, thyme,
    parsley, oregano tied together and
    removed before serving the soup)

1 10-ounce can tomato sauce
1/4 cup brandy
pinch of cayenne
salt to taste

1. Bring the water to a boil. Add bouillon cubes, garlic, and bouquet garni. Cover and allow to cook over low heat for 1 hour or more. Add more water if necessary.

2. After 1 hour of slow cooking, add the tomato sauce, brandy, cayenne, and salt. Stir, making sure to mix well. Strain and discard the garlic and bouquet garni. Serve hot during the cold months or refrigerate and serve cold during the warm months.

Broccoli Soup

Ingredients   *4 servings*

1 pound broccoli
3 garlic cloves
6 cups water
6 parsley sprigs
4 strips lean bacon

6 tablespoons olive oil
1 6-ounce can tomato paste
salt and pepper to taste
Gruyère or Parmesan cheese, grated

1. Wash the broccoli thoroughly. Slice it in small pieces, discarding the tough part of the stalks. Chop well the garlic, parsley, and bacon.

2. Pour the olive oil into a soup pot, add the broccoli, garlic, parsley, and bacon, and sauté them for a minute or two while stirring at the same time. Add the tomato paste and 2 cups water. Stir well. Cover the pot and allow the soup to cook for about 5 minutes.

3. Add the remaining water and cook the soup over medium heat for about 30 minutes. Add salt and pepper and simmer for a few minutes. Just before serving, purée the soup in a blender. Soup can be served hot or cold. If it is served hot, garnish the soup at the last minute with some grated cheese.

This is a very quick and easy soup to prepare, and an all-time favorite among our monastery guests. It can be served at any time of the year. When served cold, it should be refrigerated for at least 2 hours, and instead of the grated cheese, one may add 1 teaspoon of sour cream to each serving bowl as garnish.

Soupe Pelou

(Radish Greens Soup)

Ingredients   *4 servings*

¹/₃ cup olive oil	5 cups water
2 leeks or onions, chopped	salt and pepper to taste
1 bunch fresh radish tops and leaves	¹/₄ teaspoon nutmeg
(or mustard or turnip greens)	¹/₂ cup milk
4 potatoes, peeled and cubed	croutons as garnish

1. Pour the olive oil into a pot and add the leeks. Sauté lightly over low-medium heat for 3 minutes. Add immediately the well-washed and chopped radish tops. Stir. Cover the pot, and let the sautéing process continue for another 3 minutes.

2. Add the potatoes, water, salt, pepper, and nutmeg and stir again very well. Cover the pot and simmer the soup for 45 minutes. Allow the soup to cool.

3. Pass the soup through a sieve or blend it in a blender, and then return it to a clean pot. Add the milk and mix well. Reheat the soup if you wish to serve it hot, or refrigerate it for a few hours and serve cold.

Parsley Soup

Ingredients

4 servings

4 medium tomatoes
5 tablespoons olive oil
1 leek, finely chopped
1 onion, chopped and minced
4 garlic cloves, minced

1 cup white dry wine
4 1/2 cups water
salt and pepper to taste
1 big bunch parsley (finely chopped,
    preferably the leafy Italian type)

1. Wash the tomatoes. Boil them for a few minutes and then peel. Slice them lengthwise and discard the seeds.

2. Pour the olive oil into a soup pot. Add the leek and onion and sauté for a few minutes, until they begin to turn golden. Add the tomatoes, garlic, wine, water, salt, and pepper. Allow to boil over low-medium heat for 20 minutes. Add the parsley and continue cooking for another 10 minutes. Blend the soup in a blender. Serve hot or refrigerate for a few hours and serve cold.

"Parsley is most frequently used either chopped or in the leaf as a garnish for dishes, but it is delicious when used in large quantities as a pronounced seasoning. Like mint, it is one of the easiest of herbs to grow. Generally, there are two kinds of parsley available, the curly variety and the flat leaf, which is also called Italian parsley. Raw parsley is said to sweeten the breath."

—C. Claiborne, *An Herb and Spice Cook Book*

Gazpacho

4 large tomatoes, peeled, seeded, and coarsely cut up

2 cucumbers peeled, seeded, and coarsely cut up

1 large green pepper

2 red onions, coarsely cut up

8 cups water

4 minced garlic cloves

$^1/_3$ cup finely chopped parsley

2 slices stale bread, crumbled

$^1/_2$ cup olive oil

2 tablespoons finely chopped celery leaves

salt and fresh ground pepper to taste

1 cup dry sherry

2 tablespoons red wine vinegar

1. Prepare tomatoes and place on a separate plate. Prepare the cucumbers, sprinkle with salt, and place on a separate plate. Dice the green pepper and 1 of the red onions and place each on a separate plate.

2. Bring the water to a boil in a large soup pot, adding half the diced tomatoes, the other red onion, minced garlic cloves, parsley, stale bread, olive oil, celery leaves, and salt and pepper. Let it boil over medium heat for about 30 minutes. Cool it and add the dry sherry and vinegar and blend the soup in a blender. Refrigerate for about 4 hours.

3. When it's time to serve the soup, pass around individual plates with the diced tomatoes, pepper, cucumber, and onion. They can be added individually according to taste.

Garden Borscht

2 tablespoons oil

2 carrots, diced

1 onion, diced

1 10 1/2 can vegetable juice

5 1/2 cups water

1 1/2 pounds beets, peeled and
    coarsely shredded

2 celery stalks, thinly sliced

1 6-ounce can tomato paste

3 tablespoons sugar

2 tomatoes, peeled and chopped

1/4 cup cider vinegar

2 teaspoons salt

sour cream as garnish

1. Put the oil into a large soup pot. Cook the celery, carrots, and onion over medium heat until tender, stirring frequently. Add the vegetable juice, water, and the remaining ingredients except the sour cream. Bring the soup to a boiling point, then reduce heat to low.

2. Cover and simmer for 50 minutes or until the vegetables are tender. Stir often. Refrigerate and serve cold.

3. Just before serving, put a dash of sour cream in the center of the soup.

Borscht originated among the Russian peasants, and there are hundreds of varieties of this soup. This particular version is well adapted for summertime, and it should be chilled for several hours before serving. The classic borscht is a robust thick soup where vegetables, especially beets, are the main staple. In the summer, I use freshly picked beets from our garden for extra-special flavor.

Consommé Belle Fermière

(Farmer Vegetable Soup)

Ingredients   *4–6 servings*

3 quarts water (more if needed)   4 bouillon cubes
1 small head cabbage   8 tablespoons olive oil
1 large onion   1 bay leaf
2 carrots   salt and pepper to taste
10 French-cut string beans

1. Bring the water to a boil in a soup pot. Add the vegetables sliced in small pieces. Add the bouillon cubes, oil, bay leaf, salt, and pepper to taste.

2. After 1 hour and 15 minutes of slow cooking, turn off the heat and let the consommé sit, covered, for 15 to 20 minutes. Drain the vegetables, pour the consommé back into the pot, and bring to a boil. Serve hot, or refrigerate for several hours and serve cold.

Potage Crécy

(Carrot Potage)

10 carrots
1 potato
1 onion
8 cups water (or vegetable stock)
1 cube vegetable bouillon (if stock
    not used)

1 tablespoon tomato paste
1 tablespoon butter
1 teaspoon sugar
salt and pepper to taste
2 tablespoons heavy cream (optional)
1 tablespoon chopped parsley

1. Slice the carrots, potato, and onion. Put them into the soup pot, add the water, bouillon, tomato paste, butter, and sugar. Stir well and cook slowly, covered, over low heat for about 1 hour.

2. When the soup is done, pour it through a strainer, gently rubbing the vegetables through it. (Or blend in a blender).

3. Reheat the soup. Add salt, pepper, and heavy cream. Stir thoroughly. Serve the soup immediately, garnishing the top with parsley.

In France, the carrots grown in the vicinity of Crécy have the reputation as the best and the tastiest in the whole country — hence the name given to the soup. From France, the soup crossed the Channel into England, where it has become part of the national folklore. According to an old tradition dating back to the 14th century, loyal Britons should eat carrot soup or "potage de Crécy" on the anniversary (August 26, 1346) of the battle of Crécy, a legendary victory of the English over the French in the Hundred Years' War.

Cold Zucchini Soup

Ingredients   *4–6 servings*

6 medium-sized zucchinis $^1/_2$ cup pesto
1 leek   1 8-ounce container plain yogurt
1 teaspoon salt   fresh basil leaves and extra yogurt as
5 cups water   garnish
3 tablespoons lemon juice

1. Slice the zucchinis thinly and the leek julienne style. Place them in a soup pot, add the salt and water, and bring them to a boil.

2. Boil the vegetables for about 10 minutes and simmer them for another minute. Allow the soup to cool, then add the lemon juice, pesto, and yogurt.

3. Blend the soup in the blender. Refrigerate until the time of serving. Serve soup chilled, with 1 teaspoon of yogurt at the center, surrounded by leaves of fresh basil as garnish.

I have served this soup many times as an appetizer during midsummer when the first tender zucchinis begin to arrive in the garden, and when there seems to be an abundance of basil, of the several varieties our garden produces unfailingly. The soup always receives glowing approvals. For this particular recipe, I like to use the lemony kind of basil, which enhances the flavor of the soup.

Spicy Carrot and Orange Soup

Ingredients

6 servings

6 tablespoons olive oil
2 leeks (white part only), finely chopped
12 carrots, peeled and chopped
6 cups vegetable or chicken stock
$^1/_2$ teaspoon nutmeg
$^1/_2$ teaspoon paprika

pinch each cayenne and ginger
$^1/_2$ cup fresh cilantro, finely chopped
rind of 1 orange
$1^1/_2$ cups orange juice
salt and pepper to taste
6 thin orange slices as garnish

1. Pour the oil into a good-sized soup pot and gently sauté the leeks for about 2 minutes with the pot covered. Add the chopped carrots, stir well, cover the pot, and continue cooking for about 4 to 5 minutes over low heat.

2. Uncover the pot, stir once more, and add the stock, nutmeg, paprika, cayenne, ginger, cilantro, orange rind, orange juice, salt, and pepper to taste. Bring the soup to a boil. Cover the pot and let the soup simmer for 30 to 40 minutes.

3. Allow the soup to cook and then pass it through a sieve or blend in a blender or food processor. This soup can be refrigerated for a few hours and served cold, or if you decide to serve it hot, reheat it just before serving and let the soup stand for 3 minutes. Garnish the soup with thin orange slices at the center of each serving.

124

Wild Rice Soup

Ingredients 4 *servings*

4 cups vegetable or chicken broth
1 cup dry sherry
$^1/_2$ cup water
3 shallots, finely chopped
$^1/_2$ cup mushrooms, sliced
1 cup wild rice

salt and white pepper to taste
$^1/_2$ cup light cream
$^1/_2$ cup chopped chervil or parsley
2 teaspoons freshly chopped thyme
pinch of dry mustard

1. In a soup pot, pour the broth, sherry, and water and bring to a light boil. Add the shallots, mushrooms, wild rice, salt, and white pepper. Reduce the heat to medium. Cover the pot and cook slowly for 35 to 40 minutes.

2. Check to see that the rice is well cooked; if not, cook for another 5 minutes or so. Check the seasonings also. Add more broth if necessary.

3. Add the cream, chervil, thyme, and pinch of dry mustard. Stir the soup thoroughly. Cover the pot and simmer the soup for another 10 minutes. Serve immediately, or refrigerate it for 2 hours and serve cold.

"The making of a good soup is quite an art, and many otherwise clever cooks do not possess the tour de main necessary to its successful preparation. Either they over-complicate the composition of the dish, or they attach only minor importance to it, reserving their talents for the meal itself, and so it frequently happens that the soup does not correspond to the quality of the rest of the dishes; nevertheless, the quality of the soup should foretell that of the entire meal."

—Mme. Seignobos, *How to Train a Cook*

September

"There is no need to bewail the declining year.
Autumn is a glorious season in its own right,
and as pleasant as summer to spend in the garden.
The weather has to remain kind for this to come true,
but the same can be said of any month or season. . . .
A gale in September may leave sad,
tattered remnants in its wake,
but if the weather mends, the garden still retains
enough resilience itself to mend."

—Christopher Lloyd

Cream of Celery Soup

1 garlic clove
6 celery stalks from the heart
2 leeks or onions
2 potatoes

7 cups water
1 cup white sauce
salt and pepper to taste
chopped dill as garnish

1. Wash, peel, and trim the vegetables. Slice them into thin pieces. Pour the water into a large pot, add the vegetables, and cook slowly, covered, over medium heat for 45 to 60 minutes. Add more water if necessary.

2. In a medium-sized pot, prepare 1 cup of white sauce (see recipe p. 194).

3. After the vegetables are cooked, blend the soup in a blender and pour it back into the pot. Add the white sauce and seasonings according to taste. Stir well. Serve hot. Use dill or celery leaves chopped finely as garnish. If served cold, refrigerate the soup for a few hours before serving.

This cream of celery soup is easy to prepare and can be served hot or chilled according to the season of the year. The fresh dill garnish adds flavor and distinction to the soup.

Monastery Quick Vichyssoise

Ingredients *4–6 servings*

4 tablespoons butter, margarine, or
  oil of choice

4 leeks, finely sliced

4 potatoes, diced

1 bouquet garni (1 bay leaf, 1 sprig
  of thyme and parsley tied together
  and removed before serving the
  soup)

3 bouillon cubes (if stock not used)

3 cups water (or vegetable stock)

2 cups milk

salt and fresh pepper to taste

1 cup heavy cream or half-and-half

fresh parsley or mint leaves for
  garnish (optional)

1. Melt the butter in a large soup pot. Add the sliced leeks and cook them over low heat for about 5 to 6 minutes or until they are tender. Add the potatoes, bouillon, bouquet garni, milk, salt, pepper, and water or stock (you can add more water if necessary).

2. Raise the heat to medium and allow the soup to cook slowly, covered, for 25 to 30 minutes, then simmer for 10 more minutes. Remove the bouquet garni and blend the soup in a blender until thick and creamy. Chill the soup for a couple of hours in the refrigerator. Just before serving, pour the heavy cream into it and stir thoroughly. Serve the soup cold and garnish each plate with finely chopped parsley or mint leaves.

Potage du Jardin

(Garden Vegetable Soup)

Ingredients   *4–6 servings*

2 quarts water (or vegetable stock)   1 celery stalk
2 bouillon cubes (if stock not used)   3 Swiss chard or cabbage leaves
1 onion $1/2$ cup pastina
1 zucchini   salt and pepper to taste
1 carrot   6 tablespoons grated Gruyère cheese

1. Cut the vegetables into small slices julienne style.

2. Place the water in a soup pot. Add the bouillon cubes and vegetables and cook over medium heat for 40 minutes.

3. Add the pastina, salt, and pepper and continue cooking for another 10 minutes.

4. Serve soup hot, and sprinkle grated cheese on top of each serving.

"Gourmet cooking means food that truly satisfies the server: food in which the balance of texture and flavor is exactly right, food that looks and tastes delicious. And contrary to what many people believe, such foods do not have to be elaborate."

— Rose Elliot, *The Festive Vegetarian*

Russian Cream of String Bean Soup

Ingredients   *6 servings*

½ pound string beans, fresh or
   frozen
2 leeks, sliced
4 potatoes, peeled and sliced
3 tablespoons butter or margarine
6 cups water

2 cups milk
salt and pepper to taste
string beans cut and cooked
   separately as garnish
finely cut or chopped chives
   (optional)

1. Wash and clean the string beans, removing the ends and strings. (Use frozen beans if you don't have fresh ones.) Prepare the leeks and potatoes.

2. In a large pot, melt the butter and sauté the vegetables for 1 minute. Stir often. Add the water and bring to a boil. Lower the heat to low-medium, cover the pot, and cook the soup slowly for about 40 minutes.

3. When the vegetables are cooked and tender, pass the soup through a sieve or blend it in a blender. Return the soup to the pot and add the milk and seasonings. Stir the soup well and bring it again to a light boil. Turn off the heat and let the soup stand for 10 minutes. Serve the soup hot, and garnish it with small cut string beans that have been cooked separately. Some finely chopped or cut chives may be sprinkled on the soup.

Tomato Bouillon

Ingredients

4 servings

6 tablespoons oil of choice
6 tomatoes, peeled
1 minced onion
1 bay leaf
2 peppercorns
1 celery stalk, thinly sliced

2 tablespoons butter
2 tablespoons flour
8 cups water
salt and pepper to taste
heavy cream (optional)

1. Pour the oil into a soup pot. Add the peeled tomatoes, onion, bay leaf, peppercorns, and celery. Cook slowly (about 15–20 minutes) over low heat until vegetables are cooked. Remove the bay leaf and put the vegetables through a sieve or blend in a blender.

2. Melt the butter in the soup pot, add the flour, and mix well. Add the vegetable mixture, water, salt, and pepper. Heat to a boiling point while stirring from time to time, then let simmer for 10 minutes. Serve the bouillon hot, adding, if you wish, 1 teaspoon heavy cream to each serving.

"To make a bouillon, one needs time, because quick boiling will not extract the juices and flavors of meats and vegetables: cooking must proceed slowly and be attended to with care."

—F. L. Flagg, *A Paris Cook Book*

Cream of Corn Soup

Ingredients   *4 servings*

3 cups milk
1 1/2 cups cooked whole-kernel corn
1 large onion, chopped
1 1/2 cups cooked potatoes
1 teaspoon lemon juice

1/8 teaspoon Tabasco sauce (more or
   less according to taste)
1 cup light cream
1/4 teaspoon marjoram
salt and white pepper to taste

1. Pour the milk into a blender. Add the corn, onion, potatoes, lemon juice, and Tabasco sauce. Mix in a blender at high speed for a few seconds.

2. Pour the contents of the blender into a soup pot and bring to a boil while stirring continually. Add the cream and seasonings. Stir well and simmer for a few minutes before serving.

"Never blow your soup if it is too hot,
but wait until it cools.
Never raise your plate to your lips,
but eat it with your spoon."
— C. B. Hartley, *The Gentleman's Book
of Etiquette*

Tomato Soup Florentine Style

Ingredients

4 servings

1/2 cup olive oil
1 large onion, finely sliced
7 medium-sized tomatoes, peeled
  and chopped
2 garlic cloves, minced
1 celery stalk, thinly sliced
2 carrots, thinly sliced
2 tablespoons fresh basil, chopped

1 bay leaf
1 teaspoon thyme (or fresh)
2 bouillon cubes
6 cups water (or chicken stock)
1 bunch fresh spinach, chopped (or
  1 package frozen spinach)
salt and pepper to taste
Parmesan or Romano cheese, grated

1. Heat the oil and add the onions and tomatoes. Sauté the vegetables slightly for 3 to 4 minutes. Add the garlic cloves, celery, carrots, basil, bay leaf, and thyme. Stir well and continue sautéing for another 2 minutes.

2. Add the bouillon cubes and water or the stock and bring the soup to a boil. Cover the pot and simmer the soup for 50 to 60 minutes. Remove the bay leaf.

3. Add the spinach, salt, and pepper and continue cooking for another 10 minutes. Stir well. Turn off the heat, and let the soup stand, covered, for 5 minutes. Serve hot and sprinkle some grated cheese on top.

Fennel, Zucchini, and Tomato Soup

1 large onion, chopped
1/3 cup olive oil
4 garlic cloves, minced
2 fennel bulbs, thinly sliced
2 medium-sized zucchinis, diced
6 tomatoes, peeled, seeded, and
   chopped

8 fresh basil leaves, finely chopped
6 cups chicken or vegetable stock (or
   water)
1 cup white wine
salt and pepper to taste
fresh basil chopped as garnish

1. Sauté the onion in olive oil until it becomes soft. Add the garlic and continue sautéing for another minute over medium heat.

2. Add the fennel, zucchinis, tomatoes, and fresh basil. Stir well, reduce the heat to low-medium, and continue to sauté for 2 or 3 minutes, watching that it does not stick to the bottom of the pot.

3. Pour the stock or water into the vegetable mixture. Add the wine and bring the soup to a boil. Stir well. Cover the pot and cook slowly for 30 minutes. Add the salt and pepper, stir again, and simmer the soup for 10 minutes more. Serve the soup hot. Garnish the top of each serving with fresh basil, finely chopped.

This recipe is quintessentially Italian, inspired as it is by the cuisine of Northern Italy, where fennel, zucchini, and basil are basic everyday ingredients in cooking. The soup has a light, subtle licorice flavor given by the fennel, and for those who love fennel, it is absolutely delicious. It can be prepared all year round, but it should be made particularly during the summer and harvest months when the ingredients can be picked fresh from the garden.

Provençal Rainbow Soup

Ingredients   *4–6 servings*

1 onion   8 leaves fresh mint
2 cloves garlic   4 teaspoons olive oil
1 red pepper $1/4$ pound bacon, cut in small pieces
2 small zucchinis   6 tomatoes, peeled and seeded
20 green beans   1 quart chicken stock
1 4-ounce can pitted black olives   1 quart water
2 anchovy filets   salt and pepper to taste

1. Peel the onion and garlic and slice them finely. Cut the red pepper and the zucchinis in small cubes. Cut the green beans into three or four parts. Slice the black olives. Put the anchovy filets and the mint leaves through a food processor or blend in a blender.

2. Pour the olive oil into a large soup pot. Add the bacon, onion, and garlic and cook for 3 minutes over medium heat. Add the other vegetables, olives, and anchovy-mint mixture. Reduce the heat to low and continue cooking for 8–10 minutes, stirring from time to time.

3. Add the sliced tomatoes, chicken stock, water, salt, and pepper. Cover the pot, raise the heat to medium, and let the soup come to a boil. Cook for 20 minutes. Turn heat down and let the soup simmer for another 10 minutes. Serve hot.

This potage has all the charm and wonderful aroma that one associates with the native dishes of the rich land of Provence. The variety of colors in the vegetables, which include black olives, is the origin of the soup's charming name. This variety adds not only color, but also taste and texture to the soup. It is an interesting potage to try and experiment with.

Gumbo Potage à la Creole

$^1/_3$ cup olive oil   30 green string beans, cut small
2 onions, chopped   8 okra, sliced
2 garlic cloves, chopped   1 carrot, thinly sliced
6 cups chicken or fish stock   2 tablespoons brown sugar
2 cups dry white wine $^1/_2$ cup fresh parsley, chopped
1 6-ounce can tomato paste   salt and pepper to taste

1. Pour the oil into a large soup pot. Add the onion and garlic. Sauté them over low heat for 2 minutes, stirring often — be sure the garlic does not brown.

2. Add the stock, wine, and tomato paste. Stir well, raise the heat to medium, and bring the soup to a boil.

3. Add the green beans, okra, carrot, sugar, parsley, salt, and pepper. Stir and cover the pot. Cook for 30 minutes over medium heat, then lower heat and simmer for 10 minutes more. Serve hot.

This soup comes from old Louisiana, via France, where it was transported by some local early settlers when they returned to France. The recipe henceforth has received some modifications. For instance, okra, which is not cultivated in France, was omitted altogether. In this recipe, we have reintroduced the use of okra, as well as fish stock as an alternative to chicken stock. A dash of cayenne pepper will also make the soup a bit spicier. The use of wine in the soup is a French improvement.

Curried Soybean Soup

Ingredients   *4–6 servings*

4 tablespoons olive oil
1 onion, chopped
2 carrots, peeled and cubed
2 garlic cloves, minced
2 teaspoons curry powder

$^1/_2$ teaspoon coriander powder
2 cups soybeans
9 cups vegetable or meat stock
salt and pepper to taste
chopped cilantro as garnish

1. Pour the oil into a soup pot, add the onion and carrots, and sauté them lightly for 2 or 3 minutes. Add the garlic, curry, and coriander and stir thoroughly.

2. Add the soybeans and stock and bring the soup to a boil. Reduce the heat, cover the pot, and simmer the soup for 60 minutes or until the beans are cooked and tender (they should remain solid).

3. Remove 1 cup of the beans from the soup and blend it in a blender or food processor, then return it to the soup. Add salt and pepper and stir the soup thoroughly. Serve hot, with chopped cilantro on top as garnish.

Minestra Toscana

(Tuscan-Style Minestrone)

Ingredients   *6 servings*

½ cup olive oil
1 large yellow onion, chopped
6 cups vegetable or chicken broth
2 cups white wine
1 bouquet garni (sprigs of thyme, oregano, and bay leaf, tied together)
salt and pepper to taste

2 carrots, sliced julienne style
1 red pepper, sliced julienne style
1 zucchini, diced
16 spinach leaves, finely chopped
½ cup olives (black or green, pitted)
½ cup Italian rice or equivalent
grated Parmesan or Romano cheese as garnish

1. Pour the olive oil into a large soup pot and sauté the onion slightly for about 2 minutes over medium heat.

2. Add the broth, wine, bouquet garni, salt, and pepper and bring the soup to a boil. Reduce the heat to low-medium.

3. Add the carrots, pepper, zucchini, spinach, and olives. Cover the pot and cook slowly for 1 hour. Add the rice and more broth or water if necessary, and simmer the soup for 15 to 20 minutes more. Remove the bouquet garni. Serve hot and garnish each bowl with grated cheese.

For centuries, the green virgin olive oils of Tuscany have been regarded as the best — "smooth, light, and pleasant on the tongue" said a famous chef. It is precisely these native olive oils that are the base for almost every Tuscan soup. In this soup, the olive fruit is used as well, giving a distinctive flavor, and also enhancing the blend of colors and textures. To achieve this, I recommend the use of black olives, pitted, of course, and sliced in half.

Escarole Soup

8 tablespoons olive oil
5 garlic cloves, minced
1 onion, finely chopped
1 1/2 pounds escarole, coarsely
   chopped
2 quarts water

2 bouillon cubes
1/2 cup vermicelli noodles (or other
   small pasta)
salt and pepper to taste
grated Parmesan cheese as garnish
   (optional)

1. Pour the oil into a good-sized soup pot, add the garlic and onion, and sauté over medium heat for about 3 to 4 minutes, stirring from time to time. Add the escarole and continue to stir for another 2 minutes.

2. Add the water and bouillon and cook the soup, covered, over medium heat for 25 minutes. Add the vermicelli noodles, salt, and pepper and continue cooking for another 10 minutes, stirring occasionally.

3. Turn off the heat and allow the soup to sit, covered, for 10 minutes before serving. You may sprinkle some grated cheese on top of each soup bowl.

Red Bean and Rice Soup

3 onions, chopped

3 medium-sized carrots

2 celery stalks

4 tablespoons olive oil

2 quarts water

1 16-ounce can kidney beans

1 cup rice

1 bay leaf

salt and pepper to taste

1. Slice and chop the onions, carrots, and celery. Place them in the soup pot and add the olive oil. Sauté them for 1 or 2 minutes, stirring constantly.

2. Add the water, beans, rice, bay leaf, and seasonings. Cook over medium heat, covered, until the vegetables and rice are tender. Then simmer for 15 minutes more. Remove the bay leaf.

3. Just before serving, bring the soup to another boil, stir, taste the seasonings, and serve hot.

The purpose of simmering is to cook the ingredients for a long period in order to extract the good flavor, without allowing them to break into particles that would cloud a clear soup to the point that it could not be clarified afterward because the fat and other particles had been emulsified into the broth.

October

"Suns and skies and clouds of June,
and flowers of June together,
You cannot rival for one hour
October's bright blue weather."

— Helen Hunt Jackson

Brodo alla Romana

(Broth Roman Style)

Ingredients *4 servings*

8 cups water (add more if necessary)
2 cups white wine
2 bouillon cubes
2 large onions, chopped

2 carrots, thinly sliced
3 celery stalks, finely chopped
3 tomatoes, peeled and cubed
salt and pepper to taste

1. Pour the water and wine into a soup pot. Add all the ingredients and let it boil over low-medium heat for 30 minutes.

2. Cover the pot and let the soup simmer for at least 1 hour and 15 minutes. Strain the vegetables and serve the broth hot.

This is a Roman version of the French bouillon, and in typical Italian fashion, it adds tomatoes to the French recipe. The brodo can be thickened and made more substantial by adding either pasta or rice. Garnish it with a bit of extra olive oil and some freshly chopped herbs such as basil, parsley, or thyme.

Spinach Soup

Ingredients   *4 servings*

7 cups water
1 bunch fresh spinach
1 1/2 cups sliced mushrooms
1 onion, thinly sliced
1 bouillon cube
2 tablespoons flour

1 cup milk
2 tablespoons oil of choice (or butter
  or margarine)
1 hard-boiled egg, chopped
salt and pepper to taste

1. Bring the water to a boil and add the spinach, mushrooms, and onion. Add the bouillon cube. Cook over medium heat for 30 minutes.

2. Stir the flour into the milk, mixing thoroughly. Add this mixture to the soup. Add the oil or butter, the chopped hard-boiled egg, salt, and pepper. Cook for another 10 minutes. Turn off heat and let soup stand, covered, for 5 minutes before serving.

"Rough and repetitious as some soups may be, they are nonetheless delicious if executed by a loving hand and with fresh materials."

—F. L. Stagg, *A Paris Cook Book*

Pasta and Lentil Soup

1/2 cup olive oil
1 large yellow onion, chopped
2/3 cup chopped mushrooms
4 garlic cloves, minced
8 cups water
1 pound dried lentils
2 8-ounce cans tomato paste

1 bay leaf
1/4 teaspoon ground ginger
salt and pepper to taste
1 cup small pasta shells (or pastina)
grated Parmesan or Romano cheese
   as garnish (optional)

1. Pour the olive oil into a large soup pot. Add and sauté the onions, mushrooms, and garlic over low-medium heat for about 2 or 3 minutes. Stir continually.

2. Add the water, lentils, and tomato paste. Stir well and bring the water to a boil over high heat. Then reduce heat to medium. Add the bay leaf, ginger, salt, and pepper. Stir, cover the pot, and cook the soup for 40 minutes. Remove the bay leaf.

3. Add the pasta, cover the pot, and simmer slowly for 15 minutes or until pasta is cooked. Stir again and serve immediately. Some grated Parmesan cheese may be sprinkled on top of each serving.

"To be a maker of good soups one must not only have skill and patience, but must also use good materials. . . . Soup should be palatable and nutritious. If these qualities be lacking, there will be no excuse for serving it. Knowledge and care must be applied in combining the various ingredients in order to secure results at once pleasing and healthful."

—Maria Parloa, *Miss Parloa's Kitchen Companion*

Traditional Austrian Cheese Soup

Ingredients

4–6 servings

4 tablespoons oil
2 finely sliced celery stalks
2 leeks, sliced
2 large potatoes cut into cubes
6 cups water

1 8-ounce package cream cheese cut
  into cubes
1 8-ounce container plain yogurt
salt and pepper to taste

1. Pour the oil into a soup pot, add the celery, leeks, and potatoes, stirring constantly, for about 2 minutes. Add the water and bring to a boil. Lower the heat to medium, cover the pot, and cook the soup slowly for 35 to 40 minutes.

2. When the soup is done, reduce the heat and simmer for 10 minutes, stirring from time to time. Add the cream cheese, yogurt, salt, and pepper. Stir continuously until these latter ingredients melt and blend thoroughly with the rest of the soup. Serve hot.

"Eat soup first and eat it last, and live till a hundred years be past."

— French Proverb

Saint Seraphim Soup

Ingredients

4 tablespoons butter or margarine
  (or oil or choice)
1 cup rice
7 cups boiling water
1 large carrot, grated

1 onion, sliced
1 green pepper, cut into small pieces
2 tablespoons chopped parsley
salt and pepper to taste
sprinkle of saffron

1. Melt 4 tablespoons butter in a large soup pot and add the cup of rice to it, stirring continuously for 1 or 2 minutes.

2. Immediately add the boiling water, carrot, onion, green pepper, and parsley.

3. Cook the soup over low heat, covered, for about 30 to 40 minutes, until the rice is tender. Add salt and pepper and a sprinkle of saffron for a bit of extra aroma and taste. Let the soup stand, covered, for 10 minutes and serve.

Saint Seraphim (1759–1833), a Russian monk, lived much of his monastic life as a hermit, studying Scripture and the writings of the monastic Fathers and devoting himself to continual prayer. He cultivated a garden, cooked vegetables and bread, and cared for wild animals. His life was similar to that of the Desert Fathers of 4th-century Egypt. In the last years of his life, he left the forest and dedicated himself to spiritual direction after a vision of the Virgin Mary persuaded him to do so. Numerous visitors and a community of nuns found him an insightful and compassionate spiritual father.

Soupe Savoyarde

(Savoyard Cream of Potato Soup)

Ingredients *4 servings*

5 cups chicken stock
4 large potatoes, peeled and sliced
2 1/2 cups milk
4 tablespoons butter

2/3 cup grated Gruyère cheese (or
  Parmesan)
Salt and pepper to taste
4 slices bread, toasted

1. Pour chicken stock into a soup pot and bring it to a boil. Add the potatoes and cook them, covered, over low-medium heat for 30 minutes.

2. Blend the soup in a blender and then pour it back into the soup pot. Add the milk, butter, cheese, salt, and pepper to taste. Mix well and continue cooking until all the cheese is melted.

3. Place a slice of toast at the center of each soup plate. Pour the hot soup on top of the toast and serve immediately.

This soup, which is easy to prepare, is particularly liked by children. The normal preparation time is about 15 minutes, with another 35 minutes of cooking time. On cold days, this soup is especially welcome at the table.

Ossobuco Soup

Ingredients   *6–8 servings*

$^1/_2$ cup olive oil

2 onions, chopped

2 carrots, peeled and cubed

1 heart of celery, thinly sliced

3 cups dry white wine

1 lemon rind, grated

3 teaspoons dry sage or 3 fresh leaves

2 teaspoons rosemary leaves

2 teaspoons thyme

3 garlic cloves

10 pitted green olives

8 cups stock (vegetable or fish)

1 cup Italian rice (or brown rice)

6 teaspoons capers

salt and pepper to taste

fresh Italian parsley, chopped, as
  garnish

1. Heat the olive oil in a good-sized soup pot, and gently sauté the onions, carrots, and celery for 3 minutes, stirring frequently. Add the wine, cover the pot, and continue cooking for about 10 minutes.

2. Put the lemon rind, sage, rosemary, thyme, garlic, and olives through a food processor. Add this mixture to the soup pot. Blend and stir thoroughly.

3. Add the stock, rice, capers, salt, and pepper as necessary. Stir and cover the pot. Cook the soup over low-medium heat for about 45 minutes. Turn off the heat and let the soup rest, always covered, for 10 minutes. Sprinkle fresh chopped parsley on top of each serving as garnish. Serve hot and pass around a bowl of grated Parmesan cheese for those who wish it.

Southern-Style Vegetable Soup

Ingredients 4-6 servings

4 tablespoons butter or margarine
1 onion, sliced
8 cups water
2 carrots, diced
$^{1}/_{2}$ cup cabbage, thinly sliced
1 celery stalk, sliced
12 string beans, cut

$^{1}/_{2}$ cup peas
2 large potatoes, diced
2 tomatoes, peeled and sliced
salt and pepper to taste
chopped parsley
1 teaspoon sugar

1. Melt the butter in a soup pot. Add the onion and sauté for 2 minutes. Add the water and all the vegetables except potatoes and tomatoes. Cook over medium heat, covered, for 30 minutes.

2. Add the potatoes, tomatoes, and seasonings and continue cooking for 10 minutes more. Simmer for 15 minutes, or until all vegetables are tender. Before serving, add the chopped parsley and mix well. Serve hot.

"Soup is delicious.
Soup is nutritious.
Soup can light the inner fire.
Soup can be hot or cold,
thick or thin.
Soup is healthy,
light and stimulating—
agreeing with almost everyone."

—Bernard Clayton, Jr., *The Complete
Book of Soups and Stews*

Beet Soup

Ingredients   6–8 servings

4 beets, peeled and diced   6 teaspoons olive oil
2 onions, finely sliced   2 teaspoons sugar
3 celery stalks, finely sliced   salt and pepper to taste
2 quarts water   mixed herbs (dill and scallion tops)
1 bouillon cube   croutons (optional; see recipe p. 195)

1. Pour the water into a soup pot and add the sliced vegetables, bouillon cube, oil, and sugar. Begin to cook slowly.

2. After 30 minutes, add salt and pepper and continue cooking slowly for another 10 minutes. Let the soup stand for 15 minutes. Blend the soup in a blender and return it to the pot. Reheat for five minutes.

3. Just before serving, add the mixed herbs and ladle the soup into individual dishes. Garnish the soup with a few croutons in the center of each serving.

Beets are not an easy vegetable to deal with. Though many people like them, there are just as many, if not more, who dislike them. Often, this has a little to do with their color or taste. Beets actually taste quite good, especially when combined with other ingredients like onions.

This soup is quite simple to prepare. It is very important to slice the beets very thin and cut them into small pieces.

Soupe au Pistou

(Provençal Vegetable Soup with Pesto Sauce)

Ingredients   *6–8 servings*

2 cups dried white or flageolet beans

10 cups water

2 leeks, or onions, chopped

2 carrots, peeled and sliced

3 potatoes, peeled and cubed

2 zucchinis, cubed

12 string beans, cut into small pieces

3 tomatoes, peeled and chopped

1 stalk of celery, chopped

sprig of parsley, chopped

salt and pepper to taste

Pistou Sauce:

7 garlic cloves

10 basil leaves

1 cup olive oil

6 tablespoons grated Parmesan
  cheese

1. Soak the beans overnight in cold water. Drain them and place them in a large soup pot with at least 10 cups fresh water. Add all the vegetables and herbs and bring the water to a boil. Cover the pot and simmer the soup for about 50 to 60 minutes, or until beans are tender.

2. Add salt and pepper. Stir well and continue simmering for another 10 to 15 minutes. Keep the soup hot and covered until you are ready to serve it.

3. While the soup is simmering, prepare the *pistou* sauce as follows: Mash the garlic cloves in a mortar. Add the basil leaves and continue mashing or pounding with a pestle until they are well mixed. Add the grated cheese and mix well until it turns into a stiff, consistent paste. Place the mixture in a good-sized serving bowl and add the olive oil little by little. Mix well until it reaches an even consistency. (The *pistou* sauce can also be prepared in a blender or food processor).

4. Serve the soup hot. Pass the *pistou* bowl around, and let each person add the sauce to his or her own plate.

Those who prefer a thicker soup may add a half cup of vermicelli noodles.

Leek and Potato Soup

Ingredients

6 servings

4 tablespoons butter or margarine or oil of choice

8 leeks, cut into small, round slices

8 cups water

5 large potatoes, peeled and diced

salt and pepper to taste

chervil or parsley

1. Melt the butter in a large soup pot and add the leeks. Sauté for about 3 minutes, then add the water and diced potatoes. Cook over medium heat, covered, for about 50 to 60 minutes.

2. Add salt and pepper and mash the potatoes in the soup pot. Stir the soup well. As you dish out each serving, sprinkle a bit of minced chervil or parsley on top. Serve the soup hot.

"Well did he love garlic, onions, and eke leeks, and for to drinken strong wine, red as blood."

—Geoffrey Chaucer, *Canterbury Tales*

French Cream of Lentil Soup

Ingredients

4 tablespoons olive oil
2 bacon strips, diced
2 leeks, chopped
2 carrots, sliced
1 1/2 cups lentils
8 cups water
1 bay leaf
1 sprig thyme

chopped parsley
salt and pepper to taste
1 egg yolk
1/2 cup milk
olive oil
4 garlic cloves, chopped
croutons sautéed in the garlic and oil
  as garnish

1. Pour the oil into a soup pot, add the diced bacon, and sauté for about 2 minutes until the bacon becomes crisp. Add the leeks and carrots to the bacon mixture. Stir thoroughly and continue the sautéing process for another 2 minutes.

2. Add the lentils, water, bay leaf, thyme, parsley, salt, and pepper. Bring the water to a boil, cover the pot, and let the soup simmer over low heat for 1 1/2 hours. In the meantime, place the egg yolk in a deep bowl, add the milk, and blend well with a mixer. Put this mixture to the side.

3. Let the soup cool. Remove the bay leaf and thyme. Then pass the soup through a sieve, or blend in a food processor or a blender. Return the soup to a clean pot and reheat it. When the soup is hot, add the egg mixture. Stir and blend well. Keep the soup covered.

4. In a small frying pan, pour some olive oil and sauté the chopped garlic for a quick minute, stirring continually. Let garlic get golden, but do not let it burn. Add this garlic mixture to the soup. Stir and blend thoroughly. Serve hot, adding some garlicky croutons on top of each serving as garnish.

Corn Soup

Ingredients   *4 servings*

2 onions
2 garlic cloves
4 tablespoons lard or vegetable oil
5 cups vegetable or chicken broth (or
    water and 2 bouillon cubes)
1 red pepper, sliced in small cubes

1 green pepper, sliced in small cubes
3 tablespoons tomato paste
1 8-ounce package frozen whole-
    kernel corn
salt and pepper to taste

1. Peel, slice, and mince the onion and garlic. Melt the lard in a good-sized pot. Sauté briefly the onion and the garlic, until they begin to turn brown.

2. Add immediately the broth (or water and 2 bouillon cubes). Add the red pepper, cover the pot, and bring the contents to a boil. Lower to medium heat and cook the soup for 15 minutes.

3. After 15 minutes of cooking, add the remaining ingredients: green pepper, tomato paste, corn, salt, and pepper. Stir the soup several times until all the ingredients are well mixed. Cover the pot and continue cooking for another 15 minutes. Serve hot.

November

"Come, ye thankful people, come
Raise the song of harvest-home!
All be safely gathered in,
Ere the winter storms begin;
God, our Maker, doth provide
For our wants to be supplied;
Come to God's own temple come,
Raise the song of harvest-home!"

—Thanksgiving Hymn

Okra Soup

Ingredients

1 onion, chopped
1 1/2 cups okra, sliced
2 celery stalks, chopped
8 cups water
2 bouillon cubes

1/4 cup rice
1/2 cup corn kernels
1/2 cup tomato juice
salt and pepper to taste
pinch of cayenne

1. Put vegetables into the soup pot and add the water. Bring the water to a boil and add the bouillon, rice, corn, tomato juice, and seasonings. Stir well.

2. Cover the pot and cook the soup slowly over low-medium heat for at least 1 hour, stirring from time to time. Then simmer for 15 minutes, check the seasonings, and serve hot.

"To make nutritious, healthful and palatable soup, with flavors properly commingled, is an art which requires study and practice, but it is surprising from what a scant allotment of material a delicate and appetizing dish may be produced."

— *The Buckeye Cookbook*

Potage au Potiron

(Pumpkin Soup)

Ingredients   *6–8 servings*

6 cups water (more if necessary)
4 cups pumpkin, peeled and cubed
2 potatoes, peeled and cubed
2 carrots, large thinly sliced
2 onions, thinly sliced
2 garlic cloves, minced

pinch tarragon
salt and pepper to taste
1 quart milk
$1/3$ cup vegetable oil
$1/2$ cup parsley, finely chopped

1. Pour the 6 cups of water into a large pot. Add the pumpkin with the potatoes and the carrot and bring to a boil. Add the onion, minced garlic, tarragon, salt, and pepper and continue boiling for about 20 minutes. Reduce heat and simmer for another 20 minutes.

2. Blend the soup in a blender and then pour it back into the pot. Add the milk and the oil, stirring well, and over low heat bring the soup to a boil again. Simmer for about 10 minutes and serve immediately in well-heated soup bowls, garnishing each with a pinch of parsley.

Portuguese Kale Soup

Ingredients   6 servings

1 cup white beans
10 cups water, more if needed
2 large onions, chopped
1 pound kale, chopped
2 potatoes, peeled and cubed
1 6-ounce can tomato paste

1 teaspoon vinegar
4 garlic cloves, minced
chorizo chunks (optional: for the
    nonvegetarian)
salt and pepper to taste

1. Soak the beans overnight. Rinse in cold water.

2. Pour the water into a large soup pot and bring it to a boil. Add the beans, onions, kale, potatoes, tomato paste, vinegar, chorizo, and garlic. Cook slowly over low-medium heat for 2 hours. Add more water if necessary. Stir from time to time so the soup does not burn on the bottom of the pot.

3. When the soup is done, add the seasonings and stir the soup well. Turn off the heat, cover the soup pot, and let it stand 10 minutes before serving. Serve hot.

To say the least, this is not only a popular soup in Portugal, but also one of the better known Portuguese dishes around the world. I think it is simply marvelous that a rather common and even dull vegetable such as kale is given prominence in this soup. This, of course, is a vegetarian version of the original soup, which calls for a spicy sausage, such as chorizo, as a necessary ingredient. In my view, both versions are equally appetizing.

Black Bean Soup

2 cups black beans

4 tablespoons butter

1 onion, chopped

2 celery stalks, chopped

2 quarts water

$^1/_2$ cup rice

juice of 1 lemon

salt and pepper to taste

2 tablespoons flour

2 hard-boiled eggs, sliced

1. Soak the black beans overnight. Rinse them in cold water and drain.

2. Place 3 tablespoons butter in the soup pot, add the onion, and sauté for a few minutes. Add the beans, celery, and water. Bring to a boil, then reduce heat to low-medium. Cover the pot and cook slowly for 1 $^1/_2$ hours. Stir occasionally.

3. When the beans are tender, add the rice, lemon juice, salt, pepper, and more water if necessary. Cover the pot and cook slowly for another half hour.

4. Melt the remaining butter in a separate skillet, add the flour, and mix thoroughly. Add this mixture to the soup and blend well. When serving the soup, garnish the bowls with slices of hard-boiled eggs.

There are many recipes for black bean soup. This is a mild version of it; for the stronger and spicier Mexican-American version, add some chili peppers, garlic, cumin, and cilantro. If it is not possible to cook the beans ahead of time, a can of cooked beans may be substituted. The soup may also be garnished with a spoonful of sour cream over each portion instead of the slices of hard-boiled eggs.

Potato and Cheese Soup

3 tablespoons butter
2 leeks, thinly sliced
4 large potatoes, peeled and diced
5 cups water

2 cups milk
$1/2$ cup Cheddar cheese, grated
salt and white pepper to taste
paprika

1. Melt the butter in a soup pot. Add the sliced leeks and sauté them for about 2 minutes on low heat. Add the diced potatoes and continue sautéing for another minute while stirring continually.

2. Add the water and cook over moderate heat, covered, for 30 minutes, or until the vegetables are soft.

3. Add the milk, cheese, salt, pepper, and paprika, and bring the soup to a boil. Turn off the heat and let the soup stand, covered, for 10 minutes. Serve hot.

This is an idyllic wintry soup, both light and robust, a happy marriage between the potato and cheese. For a bit of extra strength and flavor, add 1 teaspoon of cognac per serving. Although the soup is particularly appetizing during the winter months, it is also appropriate in early spring and fall.

White Bean Soup

Ingredients   *6 servings*

1 pound dry white beans
12 cups water
2 onions
2 carrots
2 leeks
1 celery stalk
a few leaves of garden greens
   (spinach, chard, or any other
   type of green)

4 garlic cloves
6 tablespoons olive oil
2 bouillon cubes
salt and pepper to taste
finely chopped and minced thyme
   leaves

1. Soak the dry beans in cold water for at least 10 hours. Rinse them well and put them into a large soup pot with water.

2. Cut the onions, carrots, leeks, celery, and garden greens into thin pieces. Mince the garlic well. Add them all to the soup, along with the oil and the bouillon cubes.

3. Cook the soup, covered, over medium heat for about 60 minutes, stirring from time to time. Let the soup sit for about 10 minutes with the lid on.

4. Add salt, pepper, and thyme. Reheat for another 5 minutes and serve hot.

Broccoli Rabe and Bean Soup

Ingredients 4–6 *servings*

8 tablespoons olive oil
1 large yellow onion, chopped
6 garlic cloves, minced
2 potatoes, peeled and diced
4 tomatoes, peeled and chopped
3 cups precooked white beans or 2
  cans of the same beans

7 cups water
1 bunch broccoli rabe, finely
  chopped
salt and pepper to taste
fresh parsley, chopped
grated Parmesan cheese (optional)

1. In a large soup pot, sauté the onion for about a minute or two. Add the garlic and stir continually for 1 minute. Add the potatoes and the tomatoes and cook over low-medium heat for about 5 minutes, stirring often.

2. Add the precooked beans and the water and bring to a boil. Add the broccoli rabe and cook the soup, covered, over medium heat for about 30 minutes. Add salt and pepper and simmer the soup for 10 minutes. Ladle the soup into soup bowls, and sprinkle some finely chopped parsley on the top of each. Grated Parmesan cheese may be used as additional garnish.

Beans are one of the most important and healthiest staples in our everyday diet and a basic ingredient for many of the world's most delicious soups across all cultures. Beans are also a great source of protein, especially when combined with rice. The one problem faced by bean lovers is gas discomfort. This can be avoided by soaking the beans for several hours and then discarding the water in which they were soaked. Afterward cook the beans in new, clean water. This particular recipe comes from the southern Italian countryside where broccoli rabe is often used in a variety of culinary concoctions. For extra flavor, add a bouillon cube.

Zuppa alla Pavese

(Bread Soup from Pavia)

Ingredients   *4 servings*

    4 teaspoons butter or margarine   5 cups meat or stock of choice (or 5
    4 slices bread   cups water and 4 bouillon cubes)
    4 eggs   black pepper
    4 cups water   grated Parmesan cheese

1. Melt the butter in a frying pan and, over a low heat, fry the bread on both sides. Then place one slice in each soup bowl.

2. Bring to a boil 4 cups of water in a soup pot, then lower the heat. Break 1 egg at a time and place the entire egg in the boiling water for 3 minutes. With the help of a large slotted spoon, keep the egg whites all around the yolk so that the egg remains firm and whole. Place each egg on top of the bread.

3. Heat the broth (stock) in a soup pot and bring it to a boil. Ladle the stock into each bowl, covering well the bread and the egg. Sprinkle some black pepper and grated cheese on top. Serve immediately.

Rice and Ham Soup

Ingredients

4 servings

4 slices cooked ham
2 tomatoes, peeled and sliced
1 onion, sliced
4 tablespoons butter or margarine
1 cup rice
6 cups water

1 bouillon cube
sprinkle saffron
salt and pepper to taste
1 teaspoon thyme, preferably fresh
  (optional)
Romano cheese

1. Cut the ham slices in small pieces. Do the same with the tomato and the onion.

2. Melt the butter in a soup pot. Add the ham, tomato, and onion. Cook over low heat for about 2 minutes maximum. Add the rice and stir well.

3. Add 6 cups of water and the bouillon cube (or previously prepared bouillon), saffron, salt, pepper, and thyme (optional). Raise the heat to medium and cook slowly for about 30 minutes. Cover the pot and let the soup simmer for a few minutes. Serve hot, sprinkling some cheese on each serving.

Garbure Béarnaise

(Béarn Country Soup)

Ingredients   *4–6 servings*

1 pound navy beans
4 quarts water
2 leeks, cut julienne style
2 turnips, sliced
1 small carrot, sliced
1 small cabbage, coarsely chopped
20 green beans
6 potatoes, peeled and left whole

bouquet garni (1 bay leaf, 2 sprigs
   thyme, and 4 sprigs parsley, tied
   together and removed before
   serving)
6 sweet Italian sausages
2 garlic cloves, minced
1/4 pound salt pork (bacon fat)
salt and pepper to taste

1. Soak the navy beans overnight or at least for several hours. Drain and rinse them. Wash and prepare the vegetables. Pour water into a large soup pot and add all the vegetables except the potatoes, bouquet garni (bay leaf, thyme, parsley tied together), and garlic. Cover the pot and cook the soup slowly over low-medium heat for about 1 1/2 hours. Add more water as necessary.

2. Add the whole potatoes, herbs, sausages, garlic and bacon fat and continue cooking slowly for another hour and 15 minutes. At this point, taste the seasonings and add salt and pepper. (It may need very little salt because of the salt pork). Take out the whole potatoes, sausage, and pork and keep them in a warm place. Simmer the soup for 15 minutes, remove the bouquet garni, and then serve it hot, accompanied by slices of French bread.

3. After the soup, serve the potatoes and the sausages on a separate plate (1 for each person), accompanied by a fresh green salad and more slices of French bread (you may pour some vinaigrette over the potatoes).

Garbure should be served at the table steaming hot, and it should be accompanied by plenty of French bread and red wine.

Swiss Chard and Lentil Soup

Ingredients   *4 servings*

4 tablespoons olive oil
3 garlic cloves, minced
1 good-sized onion, thinly sliced
1 large carrot, cubed
1/2 cup lentils
6 cups water

1 small bunch Swiss chard leaves,
  finely chopped (8 leaves)
2 chicken bouillon cubes (or
  vegetable)
2 tablespoons balsamic vinegar
salt and pepper to taste

1. Pour the oil into a soup pot and lightly sauté the garlic, onion, and carrot until they become golden.

2. Add the lentils, water, chard, and bouillon cubes. Cover the pot and cook over medium heat for about 30 minutes.

3. Add the vinegar, salt, and pepper. Stir well and simmer the soup for about 10 minutes. Serve hot.

Basic Monastic Garlic Soup

Ingredients

6 servings

7 tablespoons oil of choice
16 large garlic cloves, minced
6 cups water or stock
1 1/2 cups white wine
salt to taste

nutmeg to taste
3 egg yolks, beaten
6 slices whole-wheat bread
3 egg whites beaten stiff

1. Pour the oil into a soup pot, add the garlic, and sauté for a few seconds while stirring constantly. Add the water, wine, salt, and nutmeg and bring to a boil. Reduce heat to low-medium and continue to cook for 30 minutes. Add the egg yolks, stirring continuously. Simmer for another 15 minutes with the pot covered.

2. When it is time to serve, reheat the soup to boiling. Place 1 slice of bread in each of the six soup bowls. Scatter the stiff egg whites over the bread, then pour 2 1/2 ladlefuls of hot soup on top of each. Serve immediately.

This recipe is a particular version of a soup popular in monasteries and convents of Latin-Mediterranean Europe (Italy, France, Spain, Portugal). Because of its monastic origins, this recipe is rather frugal in character, but it may easily be enriched by using vegetable or chicken stock prepared ahead of time, and also by adding an extra cup of wine.

Potage à l'Oseille

(Cream of Sorrel Soup)

6 tablespoons olive oil
4 leeks (chop only white parts)
1 large onion (well chopped)
6 cups sorrel, coarsely chopped
4 potatoes, peeled and cubed
6 cups water (more if needed)

2 bouillon cubes
1 bunch parsley, well chopped and
   minced
salt, pepper, and nutmeg to taste
6 tablespoons heavy cream

1. In a large stainless-steel pot, lightly sauté the leek and onion in the olive oil. Add the sorrel and the potatoes and stir for a few minutes until the vegetables are well mixed.

2. Add the water, bouillon cubes, parsley, salt, pepper, and nutmeg and boil for about 15 minutes. Simmer the soup in the covered pot for about 20–25 minutes.

3. Blend the soup in a blender and then pour it back into the pan. Add the heavy cream and stir the soup. Reheat and serve hot.

Sorrel plays an important role in French cooking since it has a good delicate flavor and color. Also, when used correctly, sorrel blends well with other flavors, adding a special richness to many recipes. I am particularly found of sorrel, not only because of its special taste, but also because of its appealing dark green color.

December

"Now Christmas is come
Let us beat up the drum,
And call all our neighbors together,
And when they appear,
Let us make them such cheer
As will keep out the wind and the weather."

—Washington Irving

Aigo-Boulido

(Herb Bouillon)

Ingredients 4 servings

8 tablespoons olive oil
2 leeks, sliced
1 onion, sliced
6 cloves of garlic, minced
2 tomatoes, puréed, seeds discarded
8 cups water
4 medium potatoes, diced
1 bouquet garni (sprigs of thyme, sage, and bay leaf tied together and removed before serving)

dash orange peel
pinch saffron (optional)
salt and pepper to taste
4 eggs
4 slices French bread
1 bunch parsley
grated cheese (optional)

1. In a large soup pot, sauté the leek, onion, and garlic in the oil. Add the tomato purée and sauté for another 2 minutes. Add water, potatoes, bouquet garni, orange peel, saffron (optional), salt, and pepper. Cover the pot. Boil for about 25 minutes, and then simmer for another 25 minutes. While the soup is simmering, poach 4 eggs in some of the broth for about 3 minutes. (Strain the soup and discard the vegetables, herbs, etc.)

2. Prepare 4 soup bowls and place a slice of French bread in the center. Ladle the soup into the bowls and place a poached egg on top of the bread. Sprinkle finely chopped parsley and cheese on top of the soup and serve hot.

"L'aigo-boulido sauvo la vido" ("The boiling water saves life") is an old Provençal saying that refers to one of the great and most popular peasant soups of Provence. Basically, it is a healing and restorative broth of vegetables and herbs. In Provence, it is the most common medicine for colds among both children and grown-ups. It is also often given when one suffers from stomach ailments.

Saint Nicholas Soup

Ingredients   *6–8 servings*

2 ounces butter or margarine

2 leeks or onions

4 medium-sized carrots

3 turnips

4 potatoes

half a medium-sized head white
   cabbage

1 teaspoon salt or more, according to
   taste

4 quarts water

croutons (see recipe p. 195)

1/3 cup minced chervil, chopped

1. Wash and peel the vegetables. Slice them into small pieces.

2. Melt the butter in a large soup pot. Add the vegetables and salt and stir a few times. Turn off the heat, cover the pot, and let it rest for about 15 to 20 minutes. Add the water and bring the soup to a boil. Reduce the heat to medium-low, cover the pot, and allow the soup to cook slowly for about 30 to 40 minutes. Stir from time to time.

3. When the soup is done, blend all of it in a blender until it becomes creamy and even. Serve hot, adding some croutons to each bowl and sprinkling some chervil on top.

Zuppa Toscana

(Tuscan Bread and Tomato Soup)

Ingredients   *6 servings*

1/3 cup olive oil
1 onion, sliced
4 garlic cloves, minced
1 tablespoon minced fresh rosemary
1 tablespoon minced sage
2 tablespoons thyme
16 slices stale French or Italian bread

8 tomatoes, peeled (or 2 16-ounce
  cans of tomatoes)
4 cups vegetable or chicken stock
4 cups dry white wine
salt and pepper to taste
grated Parmesan cheese

1. Heat olive oil in a large soup pot. Add the onion, garlic, and fresh herbs and sauté them for about 1 or 2 minutes. Do not let the onion or garlic turn brown.

2. Add the stale bread slices and continue cooking for a minute or two while stirring all the time. Turn off the heat.

3. In a separate pot, cook the tomatoes for about 4 to 5 minutes. Add the stock and the wine, salt, and pepper and bring to a boil. Lower the heat to medium-low. Add the bread mixture and continue cooking for about 12 to 15 minutes. Lower the heat and simmer for another 15 minutes.

4. Serve the soup very hot, sprinkling the grated cheese on top at the last minute.

This delicious peasant soup comes to us from the land of Tuscany. This ancient region of Italy evokes memories of the Renaissance, of art, music, fine wine, and food. This soup is typical of the region, where the abundance of olive oil, wine, and tomatoes, combined with the herbs and country bread, goes to create a most appetizing and flavorful soup. It should be prepared especially during the time of the harvest, when the fresh tomatoes are in abundance. Fresh herbs should be used as much as possible.

Saint Lucy Soup Sicilian Style

Ingredients   *6–8 servings*

4 quarts water   8 garlic cloves, minced
1 cup olive oil   2 large onions, sliced
1 pound whole-grain dried wheat   3 bay leaves
1 pound dried chickpeas   salt and pepper to taste

1. Pour the water and oil into a large soup pot. Add the other ingredients and let it boil slowly, covered, for 3 or 4 hours, stirring from time to time.

2. Check the seasonings, remove the bay leaves, and serve the soup hot. Those who wish can sprinkle some Parmesan cheese into their bowls.

This Sicilian soup is named after Saint Lucy (d. 304), one of the patron saints of Sicily. She was born of noble parents near Syracuse, and when she refused to marry a pagan young man, he denounced her as a Christian to the authorities. Sentenced to a brothel, she was made miraculously immobile. Several attempts were made to kill her, including once by fire, but the flames refused to touch her. Finally she was stabbed to death through the throat. Saint Lucy is much loved by the Sicilian people, who often give her name to their baby girls. She is also invoked by people who suffer eye trouble: Legend has it that her own eyes were torn out but miraculously restored.

Yellow Pea Soup

Ingredients   6 servings

4 tablespoons olive or vegetable oil
2 onions, chopped
1 celery stalk, thinly sliced
1 large carrot, thinly sliced
1 medium-sized turnip, diced
8 cups water

half a butternut squash, peeled and
   cut into chunks
1 1/2 cups yellow split peas
1 sprig of thyme
1 bay leaf
fresh parsley, chopped
salt and pepper to taste

1. Pour the oil into a large soup pot. Add the chopped onions and sauté them over moderate heat until the onions turn soft. Add immediately the celery, carrot, and turnip. Stir the vegetables well and continue sautéing for another minute.

2. Add the water, chunks of squash, split peas, thyme, bay leaf, and chopped parsley. Cover the pot and bring the soup to a boil.

3. Cook the soup slowly, over medium heat, for 45 to 60 minutes or until the peas are totally dissolved. Add salt and pepper. Stir well and simmer the soup for 10 minutes. Remove the bay leaf and serve hot.

The appeal of this soup lies in its taste, color, and texture. When the peas are properly cooked and totally dissolved, they turn the soup into a creamy one, yellowish in color and thick in texture. The morsels from the vegetables also enhance the texture of the soup. This soup can also be put through a food mill or a blender and served as a thick purée. The butternut squash adds a sweet, delicate flavor to the soup and enhances its yellow-orange color. For a bit of extra taste, add 1 or 2 bouillon cubes. If this soup is prepared for an elegant dinner or for a special occasion, it should be served in the creamy purée form with some fresh minced parsley on top as garnish.

Caldo Gallego

(Galician Chickpea and Sausage Soup)

Ingredients   *6 servings*

2 cups dried chickpeas or 2 15-ounce
  cans garbanzos
2 large onions, sliced
6 tablespoons olive oil
2 garlic cloves, minced
4 cups water
4 cups chicken or meat stock
1 bay leaf
1 bunch fresh parsley, chopped

1 turnip, diced
1 large carrot, diced
2 potatoes, peeled and cut in cubes
1 heart of celery, thinly sliced
8 slices sweet Spanish chorizo, cut in
  half
12 fresh spinach leaves, chopped
salt and pepper to taste

1. Soak the chickpeas overnight and then rinse them and discard the water. If you wish to save time, use the canned chickpeas (garbanzos), which taste the same.

2. In a large soup pot, sauté the onions in the olive oil for 2 or 3 minutes or until they begin to turn soft. Add the garlic and stir well.

3. Add the water and stock. Bring the soup to a boil. Add the chickpeas, bay leaf, parsley, turnip, carrot, potatoes, celery, and chorizo. Cook the soup, with the pot covered, for 1 hour and 15 minutes over medium heat or until the chickpeas are tender.

4. Add the chopped spinach, salt, and pepper and simmer the soup gently for 15 to 20 minutes, adding more water if needed. Stir it from time to time. Remove the bay leaf. Turn off the heat and serve the soup hot.

Perhaps Galicia is best known for its ancient town Santiago de Compostela, containing one of the wonders of the world: its famous cathedral, where according to tradition the Apostle James is buried.

A Hermit's Soup

Ingredients   *1–2 servings*

1 potato   3 tablespoons oil of choice
1 turnip $^1/_3$ cup rice
half a small cabbage   2 quarts water
2 carrots   salt and a pinch of thyme to taste
1 onion

1. Wash and trim the vegetables. Cut and slice all of them into tiny pieces.

2. Pour oil into a soup pot, add the vegetables, and sauté them for a few minutes. Add the rice and water. Stir well. Keeping the pot covered, cook over low heat for 1 hour. Add the salt and thyme just before serving. Stir well and serve hot.

The very nature of this soup is one of great simplicity and frugality, expressing the life of a hermit. This life is one that, in the words of Saint Paul, is "hidden with Christ in God." The hermit monk makes use of basic root vegetables for this soup, such as turnip, carrots, and onions. Added to these are the inexpensive ingredients of cabbage and rice. This soup can be made in sufficient quantities to last for a few days.

Simple Onion Soup

1 pound beef bones for stock

12 cups water

2 tablespoons flour or cornstarch

$^1/_2$ cup milk

6 onions, coarsely sliced

$^1/_2$ cup grated Gruyère, Parmesan, or
 Romano cheese

salt and pepper to taste

1. Place the bones in a large pot. Add water and bring to a high boil. Lower the heat, cover the pot, and continue boiling for 3 hours. Let the stock cool and remove the bones.

2. Take the fat from the top of the stock and place it in another casserole. Add the flour, milk, and half a cup stock. Dissolve well and cook the mixture for about 2 minutes, stirring continually.

3. Add the mixture to the soup, and also the sliced onions. Stir well and bring the soup to a second boil. Cover the pot and cook for about 30 minutes over low-medium heat. Turn off the heat, add the grated cheese, stir well, cover the pot, and let the soup stand for 5 minutes. Serve hot.

The very essence of this soup consists in its rich, long-labored, homemade stock. It blends wonderfully with the onions without overpowering the soup with a strong meaty and salty flavor. This soup is particularly welcome on a chilly day. It warms both body and soul.

Zuppa Vesubio

(Vesuvio Vegetable-Cheese Soup)

Ingredients   *5–6 servings*

7 cups vegetable or meat stock
4 potatoes, peeled and diced
4 carrots, peeled and thinly sliced
⅓ cup olive oil
2 onions

2 red peppers, diced
salt and pepper to taste
8 ounces Mozzarella cheese, as fresh
   as possible

1. Pour the stock into a soup pot and add the potatoes and carrots. Cook until the vegetables are tender. Pass the vegetables through a sieve or blend in a blender.

2. Pour the olive oil into a separate pot and sauté the onions for 3 or 4 minutes. Add the diced peppers and continue sautéing for another minute or two. Add the potato-carrot mixture and salt and pepper and cook, covered, over low-medium heat for about 20 minutes.

3. Cut the Mozzarella cheese in thin slices and add them to the soup. Ladle the soup into six bowls. Place the bowls in a hot oven (350°) until the cheese melts well into the soup. Serve immediately.

Soybean Minestra

6 tablespoons olive oil

4 ripe tomatoes, peeled

4 garlic cloves

4 parsley sprigs

2 leeks, chopped

8 leaves sorrel or spinach

10 cups water

2 potatoes, cubed

1 carrot, sliced

1 celery stalk, sliced

1 1/2 cup soybeans

10 string beans, cut small

1 ham bone (optional), or 2 bouillon
 cubes

salt and pepper to taste

1. Pour olive oil into large soup pot. Pass the peeled tomatoes, garlic cloves, and parsley through a small food processor or blend in blender. Put the mixture in the soup pot and cook slowly over medium heat.

2. Add the chopped leeks, sorrel, and 2 cups water. Bring to a boil and cook for about 10 minutes. Add the potatoes cut into cubes, the sliced carrot, celery, soybeans, string beans, ham bone, and 8 cups of water (more if needed).

3. Cover the pot and cook slowly for 1 1/2 hours over low-medium heat. Turn off the heat and add salt and pepper. Let the soup sit for about 15 minutes. Serve hot.

Soybeans are very nutritious, but they don't seem to have much flavor. However, the blend of soybeans and all the other vegetables in this soup creates a delicious and very distinctive taste, similar to a minestrone. To make a complete meal out of it, add 1 cup of rice, and for extra zest and taste, add 1 cup dry white wine.

Gloucester English Cheese Soup

4 tablespoons butter or margarine
2 leeks, shredded julienne style
2 celery stalks, sliced julienne style
2 medium-sized carrots, sliced julienne style
1 turnip, sliced julienne style
1 potato, diced
1 bouquet garni (parsley, thyme, and bay leaf tied together)

3 garlic cloves, minced
2 bouillon cubes
6 cups water
1 cup low-fat milk
salt and pepper to taste
2 cups Gloucester cheese, shredded
chopped parsley as garnish

1. Melt the butter in a large soup pot and gradually add all the vegetables. Stir well, cover the pot, and cook slowly over low heat for about 10 minutes.

2. Add the bouquet garni and the garlic cloves, stir again, and continue cooking for an additional 2 minutes. Add the bouillon cubes, water, milk, salt, and pepper. Stir thoroughly, cover the pot, and cook for 45 minutes over medium heat.

3. Turn off the heat, discard the bouquet garni, and blend the soup in a blender or food processor.

4. Return the soup to the pot. Reheat the soup at low to medium heat and add the shredded cheese. Simmer the soup for 10 minutes and serve it hot. Garnish the soup with finely chopped parsley and some extra shredded cheese.

This very tasty soup originates, as the name proclaims, from Gloucester, England, where the well-renowned Gloucester cattle produce an abundance of milk, some of which in turn is made into the famous Gloucester cheese. If this particular cheese is not available, substitute with another English cheese, preferably of the blue variety.

Beer Soup

Ingredients   *4–6 servings*

5 cans beer of choice
2 tablespoons sugar
4 egg yolks
6 tablespoons crème fraîche (or
   heavy cream)

$^1/_2$ teaspoon cinnamon
$^1/_2$ teaspoon salt
black pepper to taste

1. Pour all the beer into a large soup pot. Add the sugar and dissolve it slowly in the beer over low-medium heat. Bring to a boil and then remove the soup pot from the heat.

2. Beat the egg yolks in a deep bowl, adding the crème fraîche (or heavy cream), a little bit at a time. Add 4 tablespoons hot beer to the egg mixture and blend well.

3. Pour the egg mixture into the soup pot containing the hot beer. Add cinnamon, salt, and pepper. Reheat the soup over low heat and stir constantly. Allow the soup to cook for a few minutes without bringing it to a boil. Serve soup hot.

"Cooking is also of all the arts the one that has done most to advance our civilization, for the needs of the kitchen were what first taught us to use fire, and it is by fire that man has tamed nature itself."

—Anthelme Brillat-Savarin

Acorn Squash Soup

Ingredients   *4 servings*

2 large acorn squash   2 cups milk
1 large onion, chopped   4 tablespoons vegetable oil
1 cup rice   pinch sugar
1 celery stalk, chopped   salt and white pepper to taste
4 cups water   chopped parsley

1. Peel the squash and cut it into cubes. Place them in a soup pot and add the chopped onion, rice, chopped celery, and water. Cook the soup, covered, over medium heat until vegetables are tender.

2. Strain the soup through a sieve or blend it in a blender. Reheat soup and add the milk, oil, sugar, salt, and pepper. Stir and bring to a boil, then simmer for 2 to 3 minutes. Sprinkle with parsley just before serving. Serve hot.

This is a lovely soup for wintertime. Acorn squash keeps well in our cellars during the winter, and it is a joy to make use of them in different ways in the kitchen. The taste and texture of the acorn squash enhances the quality of the soup. If the soup is a bit too thick, add some extra water.

Egg Soup

2 large onions, chopped and minced
6 tablespoons olive oil
6 cups strong vegetable stock
2 cups dry white wine

4–6 well-beaten eggs (1 per person)
salt and pepper to taste
a pinch of cayenne (optional)
$^1/_2$ cup chopped chervil

1. Pour the oil into a soup pot, add the onions, and cook them slowly for a few minutes. Stir and do not let them get brown.

2. Add the vegetable stock and the wine. Cover the pot and bring to a boil, then simmer for 10 to 15 minutes.

3. Beat the eggs and add them to the soup. Add the salt, pepper, and cayenne. Reheat the soup, stir, but do not bring to a boil. Serve immediately and sprinkle some chervil on the top of each serving as garnish.

This is a versatile, quick, and easy-to-prepare soup. To me, it is a rather nostalgic soup, for it captures some of the fond memories of early childhood when my parents or grandparents would give us children egg soup when we were sick, so that being properly nourished, we would recover quickly. Because this is such a simple and basic soup, condiments (onions, cayenne pepper, chervil, etc.) are absolutely necessary in order to give flavor to the soup.

Mushroom Soup

6 medium-sized potatoes

20 mushrooms, preferably the dried type

4 fresh parsley springs

4 garlic cloves, minced

4 tablespoons butter or margarine

6 cups boiling water

salt and pepper to taste

10 teaspoons crème fraîche

1. Wash and peel the potatoes. Cut them into cubes. Wash and slice the mushrooms thinly and evenly. Peel and mince the garlic and parsley.

2. Melt the butter in a large saucepan. Add the potatoes and mushrooms and cook them over medium heat for about 3 minutes, stirring often. Add the garlic, parsley, salt, and pepper and mix well.

3. Add boiling water and cook the soup for 1 hour. (Add more water if needed.)

4. Just before serving, add the crème fraîche and blend thoroughly. Serve hot.

This is a delicious, easy-to-prepare, and very economical soup. If possible, one should try to use cèpes, the dried type of mushrooms that are used in France. Some of the local markets offer them from time to time. If they are not available, ordinary mushrooms will do. The same can be said for crème fraîche — if it is not available locally, you may substitute an equal amount of sour cream.

Potage aux Deux Légumes

(Celery-Carrot Soup)

Ingredients   *4 servings*

3 carrots   salt and pepper to taste
1 heart of celery   parsley as garnish
5 cups chicken stock

1. Wash and slice vegetables thinly.

2. Pour the stock into a soup pot and bring it to a boil.

3. Add the sliced vegetables, salt, and pepper, and cook over medium heat for 15 to 20 minutes. Serve hot. Sprinkle some fresh minced parsley over each plate.

This is an easy soup to prepare in an emergency situation, when one has little time to go through a more complicated recipe. It is a particularly good soup for children. I recommend that the carrots and celery be sliced thinly lengthwise, as for french-fried potatoes.

Appendix:
Basic Recipes for Stocks, Sauces, and Croutons

Meat Broth

Ingredients

about 10 cups

16 cups water (more if necessary)
2 pounds beef bones, shoulder, top
    ribs, etc. (any bones and meat that
    can be spared are good)
2 leeks, sliced
2 onions, sliced
2 carrots, sliced
1 celery stalk, sliced
2 potatoes, peeled and sliced

4 garlic cloves, minced
2 bay leaves
1 sprig of thyme (or 1 teaspoon
    dried)
4 whole cloves
8 black peppercorns
6 sprigs parsley
salt to taste

1. Pour the water into a large soup pot and add the meat, bones, vegetables, and all the spices. Bring it to a boil. Reduce the heat and simmer the broth for about 3 to 4 hours, stirring it from time to time. Cover the pot.

2. After the long simmering, when the broth is done, remove the bones and meat. Pass the broth through a thin strainer, which should collect all the vegetables and spices and leave the broth clear.

3. Serve the broth hot as such, or refrigerate and use it later as the base for other soups. It can also be put in the freezer to keep it for future use.

Consommé

Ingredients   *4 servings*

6 cups meat broth (see recipe on
   previous page)
³/₄ pound ground lean beef
1 carrot, sliced
1 leek, sliced

1 bouquet of celery leaves and
   parsley sprigs well tied
1 egg white, well beaten
salt and pepper to taste

1. Pour the broth into a large soup pot. Add the meat, vegetables, bouquet of celery and parsley, and egg white. Stir well the ingredients in the broth and bring it to a boil.

2. Lower the heat to low-medium, stir some more, add salt and pepper, cover the pot, and let the consommé cook slowly for about an hour and a half.

3. Filter the consommé through a very fine strainer or cheesecloth, and then serve it very hot. This consommé can be served as an appetizer to a very fine and elegant dinner.

Vegetable Broth

18 cups water (add more if necessary)
3 carrots, sliced
2 turnips, sliced and diced
2 zucchinis, sliced
2 leeks, sliced
1 onion, coarsely chopped
2 celery stalks, sliced

1 small lettuce, coarsely chopped (or a few leaves of cabbage)
4 bay leaves
1 orange peel, minced
a few parsley sprigs, tied together
black peppercorns to taste
salt to taste

1. Pour the water into a large soup pot and add all the ingredients mentioned above. Bring the water to a boil and keep it boiling for about 30 minutes. Stir from time to time.

2. Reduce the heat to low-medium, stir some more, cover the pot, and let the broth simmer for about 2 hours. Filter the broth through a fine sieve, strainer, or cheesecloth. Allow it to cool and then store it in the refrigerator or freezer for future use. This bouillon is a wonderful remedy in case of colds and stomach troubles.

Chicken Broth

about 12 cups

Ingredients

18 cups water
2 pounds chicken pieces (or more if available)
2 onions, coarsely chopped
2 leeks, thinly sliced
2 carrots, sliced
1 celery stalk, sliced

5 garlic cloves, minced
1 bay leaf
1 egg white, beaten
a bouquet of thyme and parsley sprigs, tied
black peppercorns to taste
salt to taste

1. Pour the water into a good-sized soup pot and add all the ingredients mentioned above. Bring the water to a boil, stir thoroughly, and then reduce the heat to low-medium. Cook slowly for about 2 hours and add more water if necessary.

2. When the broth is done, turn off the heat and let it rest gently for about 45 minutes. Withdraw the chicken and vegetables and then ladle the broth through a very fine strainer, or even better, through cheesecloth. When the broth has cooled, place it in proper plastic containers and store it in the freezer for future use.

Fish Broth

about 12 cups

Follow the recipe for Chicken Broth, but substitute fish bones, tails, etc., for the chicken pieces and add all the juice of a whole lemon. The best type of fish to use for broth making are red snapper, cod, haddock, and striped bass. It takes less time to make fish broth, so 1 1/2 hours of slow cooking is enough for the making of a fine broth or stock.

White Sauce

Ingredients   *about 1–1 1/2 cups*

    2 tablespoons cornstarch or flour   salt and black pepper to taste
    1 1/2 cups milk   dash of nutmeg
    2 tablespoons butter or margarine

Dissolve the cornstarch into a half cup of milk. Melt the butter in a medium-sized stainless-steel pot over medium heat. When the butter begins foaming, add the milk and cornstarch and stir continuously. Add the rest of the milk, salt, pepper, and nutmeg and continue to stir until the sauce comes to a boil. Lower the heat and continue stirring until the sauce thickens. The sauce is ready when it is smooth and thick. The sauce can be used as a base for many other useful variations. It can be used on fish, meats, eggs, vegetables, and soups.

Béchamel Sauce

Ingredients   *about 2 cups*

    2 tablespoons butter or margarine   1 tablespoon dry sherry (optional)
    2 tablespoons cornstarch or flour   salt and pepper to taste
    2 cups milk   pinch of nutmeg (optional)

Melt the butter in a good-sized stainless-steel pot over medium-low heat. Add the cornstarch and stir continuously with a whisk. Add the milk little by little while whisking continuously. Add the sherry, salt, pepper, and nutmeg and continue stirring. When it begins to boil, reduce the heat and continue cooking slowly until it thickens. This sauce is excellent with fish and vegetables, and it is a necessary base for soufflés, omelettes, and other egg dishes.

Croutons

Ingredients   *6 servings*

6 tablespoons olive oil
2 garlic cloves, minced
6 slices French bread (or Italian, or
   any other of your choice), sliced
   in cubes

dash each of dried thyme and dried
   parsley

1. Pour the oil into a pot, add the garlic, bread cubes, and herbs. and sauté them over low heat for 3 to 5 minutes. Stir and turn constantly.

2. Remove the croutons and keep them in a lightly warm oven until you are ready to use them. Croutons are especially useful as garnish in thick, creamy soups.

"Soup sought is good,
but given unsought is better."
— Old Proverb

Index

Artichokes, 10, 103
Asparagus, 63, 73
Avocados, 81, 108

Bacon, 116, 136, 155, 167
Barley, 14, 26
Basil, 112, 153
Beans
    Black, 27, 50, 65, 161
    Fava, 47
    Lima, 44, 50
    Red, 33, 50, 141
    String, 131
    White, 28, 50, 93, 160, 163, 164
Beer, 38, 183
Beets, 57, 120, 152
Black-Eyed Peas, 18
Bouillabaisse, 30
Bread, 45, 46, 165, 174
Broccoli, 76, 116
Broccoli Rabe, 164
Brussels Sprouts, 12, 67

Cabbage, 9, 52, 74, 82, 151, 173, 178
Carrots, 75, 94, 98, 110, 122, 124, 187
Cauliflower, 15, 92
Celeriac, 75, 102
Celery, 97, 128, 187
Champagne, 87
Cheese, 35, 147, 162, 180, 182
Cheese, Camembert (or Brie), 87
Cheese, Cheddar, 49
Chervil, 90
Chickpeas, 7, 50, 64, 175, 177
Cilantro (Coriander), 96
Consommés, 25, 102, 104, 107, 115, 121, 132,
    144, 172
Coriander (Cilantro), 96
Corn, 106, 133, 156
Cream Soups, 11, 15, 20, 29, 35, 45, 48, 54, 60,
    63, 67, 71, 73, 76, 81, 85, 92, 94, 97, 98,
    101, 103, 114, 122, 128, 129, 131, 133, 149,
    155, 159, 170, 182

Cucumbers, 91, 95
Curry, 60, 138

Eggs, 185
Endives, 84
Escarole, 28, 85, 140

Fennel, 114, 135
Fish Soups, 16, 30, 61, 86, 91, 106, 109

Garlic, 25, 43, 115, 169
Gumbo, 137

Ham, 166
Herbs, 172

Kale, 160

Leeks, 29, 129, 154
Lentils, 24, 39, 50, 155, 146, 168
Lettuce, 85, 100

Milk, 46, 55
Minestrone, 41, 56, 78, 139
Mint, 110
Mushrooms, 6, 8, 32, 38, 54, 86, 186

Okra, 137, 158
Onions, 40, 87, 179
Oranges, 73, 97, 124
Orzo, 13
Oysters, 86

Parsley, 100, 118
Parsnips, 19
Pasta Soups, 13, 34, 56, 66, 78, 93, 130, 140,
    146
Peas, 11, 71, 110, 176. See also Split Peas
Peas, Black-Eyed, 18
Peppers, 62
Potatoes, 10, 42, 58, 77, 88, 103, 129, 149, 154,
    162
Pumpkin, 159

Radish Greens, 117
Ravioli, 34
Rice, 36, 125, 139, 141, 148, 150, 166

Saints Soups: Antony, 14; Basil, 6; Bertille, 100; Christopher, 82; Germain, 80; Joseph, 64; Lioba, 38; Lucy, 175; Nicholas, 173; Patrick, 49; Scholastica, 23; Seraphim, 148
Sausage, 177
Shrimp, 61, 106
Sorrel, 59, 70, 100, 104, 170
Sour Cream, 32, 58
Soybeans, 138, 181
Spinach, 20, 85, 134, 145
Split Peas, 50, 80

Squash, 51, 184. *See also* Zucchini
Swiss Chard, 168

Tomatoes, 17, 72, 105, 107, 118, 132, 134, 135, 144, 174
Turnips, 22

Vegetable Soups, 23, 36, 41, 56, 78, 79, 89, 101, 112, 119, 121, 130, 136, 139, 148, 150, 151, 153, 167, 180. *See also* Minestrone; *listings under individual vegetables*
Vermicelli, 66

Watercress, 48, 85, 100

Zucchini, 111, 123, 135